AFFILIATE MARKETING #2020

Learn The Ultimate Mastery Secrets To Build a Passive Income With Social Media Marketing, SEO & Ads. Step by Step Beginners Guide Even For eCommerce or Dropshipping Business

Clark Ray Preace & Christopher Jake Higdon

© Copyright 2020 by Clark Ray Preace & Christopher Jake Higdon - All rights reserved.

The content contained within this book may not be reproduced, duplicated or transmitted without direct written permission from the author or the publisher.

Under no circumstances will any blame or legal responsibility be held against the publisher, or author, for any damages, reparation, or monetary loss due to the information contained within this book. Either directly or indirectly.

Legal Notice:

This book is copyright protected. This book is only for personal use. You cannot amend, distribute, sell, use, quote or paraphrase any part, or the content within this book, without the consent of the author or publisher.

Disclaimer Notice:

Please note the information contained within this document is for educational and entertainment purposes only. All effort has been executed to present accurate, up to date, and reliable, complete information. No warranties of any kind are declared or implied. Readers acknowledge that the author is not engaging in the rendering of legal, financial, medical or professional advice. The content within this book has been derived from various sources. Please consult a licensed professional before attempting any techniques outlined in this book.

By reading this document, the reader agrees that under no circumstances is the author responsible for any losses, direct or indirect, which are incurred as a result of the use of information contained within this document, including, but not limited to, errors, omissions, or inaccuracies

Introduction 9

Chapter 1. The Affiliate Marketing 11

How Does Affiliate Marketing Work? 13

How Do Affiliate Marketers Get Paid? 15

Why Be an Affiliate Marketer? 17

How to Become a Successful Affiliate Marketer 21

The Players Involved in Affiliate Marketing and Their Roles 25

Steps to Becoming an Affiliate Marketer 33

How Affiliate Marketers Get Paid 39

Choosing Affiliate Marketing Payment Models 41

Reasons Why You Need a Website 45

Chapter 2. Keyword Research 47

Keyword research 47

Types of keywords 48

Finding the right keywords for successful search engine optimization 49

The distinction between good and bad keywords .. 50

Recommendation of keyword species 52

Chapter 3. Social Media & SEO 64

Creating Your Business Goals 64

Creating Your Social Media Goals 66

Determining What Platforms Will Work Best for You
.... 69

Understanding SEO 70

Chapter 4. How to find A Niche 78

Pick a niche you enjoy 79

Micro-niche 79

Affiliate marketing 80

Monetizing 81

Final research 81

How to write your blog to sell? 82

Chapter 5. How to Structure Your Site for Easy and Automatic SEO 88

Chapter 6. Web Analytics 102

The Exponential Power of Google Analytics 103

Chapter 7. Dropshipping 105

Who is Dropshipping For?................................ 105

How does Dropshipping work? 106

Myths about Dropshipping............................... 108

Chapter 8. Passive Income and Advertising for Blogging Profit 110

Choose the Right Affiliate Marketing Program 112

An Affiliate Aggregator May Be a Good Idea 113

Create Some Content that Will Actually Sell....... 114

Integrate Affiliate Links in the Right Way 116

Chapter 9. The Most Important Tips for Success in Affiliate Marketing 118

Strategies To Generate Traffic 126

Chapter 10. Step by Step On How to Practice Affiliate Marketing 129

Reach Out to Customers Using Various Methods 129

Partner with the right affiliates........................ 130

Use promotions from many sources.................. 131

How to Make Use of Coupons, Deals, And Promotions... 133

Product Page Optimization 139

Chapter 11. Step by Step On How to Practice Social Media Advertising................................ 148

How to Create a Social Media Marketing Plan...... 151

Chapter 12. The Top Tools............................ 157

Chapter 13. The Top 9 Mistakes You Shouldn't Make in Affiliate Marketing 169

Mistake 1 – Wrong product choice..................... 169

Mistake 2 – Promoting too many products right from the beginning 171

Mistake 3 – Only trying to sell and not help........ 172

Mistake 4 – Poor quality website 174

Mistake 5 – Content that is regular and of high-quality... 176

Mistake 6 – Not keeping an eye on the performance of your website... 177

Mistake 7 – Neglecting content readability 179

Mistake 8 – Ignoring SEO 180

Mistake 9 – Not making evergreen content 180

Chapter 14. Create Your Affiliate Marketing Plan 182

Conclusion **193**

Introduction

Contrary to what most people would think, Affiliate Marketing did not start after the invention of the Internet; rather, it has been around for a lot longer than that. However, the Internet gave it the boost it needed to really take off and gain ground. Today, most people see it as something that started a decade or two back and only happens online, which might not be the truth.

If you were to ask a random user of the Internet what he or she thought Affiliate Marketing was; he or she would likely claim that it was a way of making money online as an intermediary. Here, people make a commission from a sale or a referral when a visitor to his or her site clicks on a link that directs him or her to a product or page online. However, as much as there is a lot of truth there, Affiliate Marketing does not only have to take place online. For example, affiliate marketing is also where a plumber gives a client a discount for referring him or her to a new client. It is the same concept.

This kind of marketing happens a lot in the real world, but people do not trace or coordinate it as much as is the case with online marketing. Business owners can ask their customers how they came to know about them in an effort to learn about their client base, but they cannot get as much information as they would be using online tracking.

The growing online market has made this type of marketing more popular and profitable. It has also made it easier to grow and expand whatever type of business an individual is in with the help of numerous professional marketers who will not necessarily appear on their payroll. Therefore, while its history started long before the invention of the Internet, the Internet has transformed it and made it widely available to the masses.

Chapter 1.   The Affiliate Marketing

Affiliate marketing is the arrangement whereby an affiliate earns a commission for completing an agreed-upon marketing objective. Commonly, the affiliate markets products and services belonging to a third party, and they earn a commission for each customer they bring on board. This economic arrangement has existed for as long as businesses have been around, but it became much more pronounced in the age of the internet. There are many affiliate marketers who earn six and seven figures. The beauty of affiliate marketing is that there are almost no barriers, and all you need is an internet connection, and you are good to go.

Most people who are stuck in a boring corporate job and would like to escape the rat race would do really well by crossing over to the world of affiliate marketing. As an affiliate marketer, you could even choose to work from the comfort of your home, and your earning potential will be governed by your depth of hunger for success. The hungrier you are, the more work you put in, and thus the more money that flows to your side, but if you are lazy, then expect to make little money and in some cases, no money at all. Just because affiliate marketing offers freedom doesn't mean that money will automatically flow into your bank account.

There's considerable work to be done, especially in the early stages, and then you can put up systems that will make your work all the easier. Also, the world of affiliate marketing is ever-changing, and an affiliate marketer must keep reinventing themselves so that they don't lose to their competition.

Advertising is a common theme in the world of affiliate marketing. Besides picking a profitable product, your advertising methods will play a critical role in determining your overall success. Some of the popular advertising methods include display advertisement, social media advertisement, email marketing, video advertisement, and blogging.

Most businesses have embraced affiliate marketers, as that's one of the best ways to increase business revenue and brand visibility.

As an affiliate marketer, there are key things you must pay attention to, or else you are at risk of sabotaging your efforts. The two main things you must carefully select are the product and the merchants. Working with transparent merchants ensures that your hard work doesn't go down the drain.

Affiliate marketing is one of the best ways to escape the rat race, create time for the things (and people) you care about, and, most importantly, attain financial freedom.

How Does Affiliate Marketing Work?

In order to understand how affiliate marketing works, you first have to become aware of the key players. The more understanding you have about these key players, the more your capacity to achieve your goals.

Brands: these are firms or individuals that own the product or service. The sectors are as diverse as you can imagine; retail, industry, financial services, travel, e-commerce, etc. Affiliate marketers that make the most money are affiliated with brands. They have been around for quite a while, and they understand the ins and outs of the market, and the brands can trust them for a great ROI. However, if you are starting out in affiliate marketing, best to stay away from brands, and work with affiliate networks.

Affiliates: the affiliate is the marketing partner of various brands. As an affiliate marketer, it is your job to win more customers for the product you are promoting and get compensated as per the agreement. The great thing about affiliate marketing is that you can still get started despite having little resources. For instance, if you have a blog, that's enough, and you can write reviews, post on social media, and direct your target audience to your affiliate links. Affiliate marketing can also be an expensive job, as you may need a considerable budget in order to buy ad spaces and traffic. If you have the budget, and you are good at optimizing the campaigns, this combination would net you tremendous profits.

Affiliate networks: an affiliate network pools together all brands that are looking to have their products and services promoted. And then affiliate marketers may sign up to these affiliate networks so they may promote the program that they feel they are sufficiently equipped to promote. Newbie affiliate marketers ought to sign up to affiliate networks so that they may have access to the numerous affiliate programs and thus get a chance to decide what they are best at promoting. Affiliate networks also handle the tracking, reporting, and payments, meaning that the affiliate marketer won't have trouble claiming their earnings, as there is an established method of doing things.

The affiliate marketer promotes the products or services of a brand with the primary aim of increasing business, and they get compensated as per their agreement with the affiliate network or brand.

How Do Affiliate Marketers Get Paid?

Considering there are diverse products and services being promoted, there are bound to be diverse metrics of paying the affiliate marketers. What is important is for the affiliate marketer to understand what's asked of them and align themselves with the program that promises the greatest rewards. For instance, if you run a real estate website, it would make more financial sense to sign up to an affiliate program that seeks emails belonging to potential real estate customers as opposed to signing up for an affiliate program that seeks web-hosting customers. The following are the common metrics upon which an affiliate marketer is compensated.

Pay per sale: in this case, an affiliate marketer receives a commission for every person they get to purchase a product. Affiliate networks are chock full of brands that are looking to grow their sales volume. If you have an established blog, you have a head start, and you may recommend products that are aligned to your audience, and you will see your commissions accumulating. You may also engage in media buying and target your traffic so that they will convert into customers. Ensure that you are slow and deliberate as opposed to being unpractical. Careless mistakes can cost you a fortune.

Pay per click: not every merchant is merely looking to make a sale. There are some merchants who are looking to expand their visibility. And they are ready to pay an affiliate marketer to bring targeted audience to their website. Thus, for every click you send to their website, the merchant happily pays you a commission. For some reason, affiliate marketers, especially newbies, might feel the need to take advantage of the situation and send illegitimate clicks so they may inflate their commissions, which almost always ends badly for them. Ensure that you are transparent in your efforts to earn a commission. As an affiliate marketer, you only succeed when the merchant/brand succeeds, and if you are a fraud, you are contributing to the brand's demise, and should you be successful, that's one less employer off the market. It never ends well.

Pay per lead: data is one of the most valuable elements of successful businesses, and merchants and firms are well aware of this fact. They are willing to pay affiliate marketers to collect data on their target clients. The most valuable datum is the email address. There are many affiliate programs that compensate marketers for every email belonging to a target audience that they bring aboard.

Most merchants and affiliate networks pay out commissions weekly and monthly. There might be restrictions on newbies, but once they earn a considerable amount, the restrictions are lifted. Depending on your location and the affiliate network or merchant in question, there are many ways that the affiliate marketer receives their commissions, including bank transfers, checks, and e-payment platforms like PayPal and Paxum.

Why Be an Affiliate Marketer?

Most people with corporate jobs are trapped in a rat race. They almost have no time for themselves. The biggest advantage of being an affiliate marketer is the fact that you are now free to work under your own terms. If you are feeling unwell, you can sleep in and work the following day. Conversely, if you are energetic, you may channel all your energies into marketing and boost your earnings. In the corporate world, you could work as hard as possible, but still, your salary remains the same while your employer enjoys the fruits of your hard work. The following are some of the other great reasons why being an affiliate marketer is a great thing.

It's a diverse billion-dollar industry

Think about any product or niche, and chances are there's an affiliate program catering to it. You will have more success by promoting products and services that you take great interest in. When you sign up to an affiliate network, you have the opportunity to select your favorite program from diverse offers. This ensures that you are making money while promoting products that you are passionate about.

Low-cost

Commonly, when people decide to escape their corporate job and achieve financial freedom, more often than not, they are looking to set up their own business. But then setting up and running a successful business is not an easy thing, for you need tremendous capital, which might very easily lead you down the path of debts, and the fact that upwards of 80% of startups fail within five years doesn't make the idea any more appealing. But when it comes to affiliate marketing, you don't need a lot to get started. In fact, with just an internet connection and an active social media account, you could be well on the way to receiving your first commission in a week's time.

Expertise is not a necessity

Think about being a surgeon. You have to go to school and get certified before you can start to practice. If you were found operating on someone's brain without a license, it would land you in trouble, right? Actually, these regulations are great. But when it comes to affiliate marketing, the results are the only thing that matters. You might not be very great at marketing a certain product, but as long as you are putting an effort to achieve your marketing goals, that's fine. You'd be surprised that most successful affiliate marketers have a background in totally unrelated fields.

Passive income

When you are an accountant with a big pharmaceutical, you must always show up to work to earn a salary. If you stay away from work, you presumably don't get the salary. But when it comes to affiliate marketing, you have a perfect opportunity to earn while you sleep. Of course, this won't happen automatically. You have to put in tremendous initial work so that you may be able to earn passively. For instance, if you own a blog, you have to generate valuable content so that the search engines will keep directing traffic to your blog, and the visitors will heed to your various Calls to Action. In this way, you will be earning passively. This is exactly why you see many affiliate marketers affording to tour the world and living in exotic places. They might be traveling, but they are also earning, so the party doesn't stop.

You become a thought leader

People seem to trust people that demonstrate competence. When you have been marketing a product or service for a while, you will acquire more knowledge about the product and service, and it will show in your marketing message. In that case, you qualify to become a thought leader, and people will start looking to you for guidance where that product or service is involved. Being a thought leader boosts your earning potential as you are in a position to influence more people, and you also have the luxury of setting higher prices than the norm. But then again you have to be careful that you don't abuse your power else people will become vicious with you.

How to Become a Successful Affiliate Marketer

Some people imagine that just because they have a great ad budget, they are automatically going to succeed in affiliate marketing. Having a great budget and even selecting great programs is fine, but that's not the end all be all to affiliate marketing. There are various factors you must consider in order to succeed as an affiliate marketer.

Learn to specialize

One of the biggest rookie mistakes most affiliate marketers are prone to make is the tendency of chewing more than one can swallow. Just because affiliate networks are chock full of affiliate programs doesn't mean that you are at liberty to promote every last one of them. The programs are mainly diverse for the purpose of letting you choose from a wide array. Thus, always ensure that you are promoting a few products that are centered on your circle of competence. When you promote too many programs, you are bound to become overwhelmed and lose motivation. Also, you could lose a lot of time and money. But when you specialize in a certain niche, you are in a position to maximize your earnings, and possibly become a thought leader.

Use several traffic sources

Some affiliate marketers seem to have a fixed mindset as to which traffic sources are the best. Maybe they ran a successful campaign using native ads and developed a fondness toward native ads, so much, so they always use native ads for all campaigns. As an affiliate marketer, you must have an adventurous spirit and test out the effectiveness of various traffic sources. Of course, you may lose some money, but in the end, you will gain great insight as to what types of traffic sources are the best for various offers.

Track your affiliate campaign

If you are not careful, you could lose a lot of money, especially when you engage in media buying. Don't just throw your affiliate link and pray that the commissions should start rolling in. You want to track your campaign results and ensure that there are no glitches, and should you find one, waste no time in correcting it.

Research

Common sense dictates that you stand the best chances of making a profit when you promote a product in high demand. But then you can only understand the popularity of a product by conducting research. Some marketers rush into promoting shiny products only to make losses. Always ensure that you engage in research so that you maximize your earnings.

Stay aware

The marketing trends of the early 2000s are not similar to marketing trends today. The only thing constant in life is change. In the world of affiliate marketing, you must keep an eye on the changing trends and learn to adapt, or else you will lose out to your competition. You don't want to be in a position that you are forced to change. You want to discern the changes and make yourself flexible. This ensures that you are always ahead of the pack. And it guarantees that you are always running profitable campaigns.

Be creative

In as much as it is important to keep up with the marketing trends, it is just as important to be creative. When we talk about creativity, we don't mean to say that you should invent the next commercially successful computer. But creativity means that you should deliver your marketing message from a creative angle. People are extremely responsive to creativity. A creative message triggers certain emotions in your target audience and increases the likelihood of them converting into customers.

Select the right merchants

You can only become successful in affiliate marketing when you are dealing with a trustworthy affiliate network or merchant. You'd be amazed by the fraudulent practices of various brands and affiliate networks. When you fall in the hands of a scamming merchant, your hard work will go down the drain, and you won't be compensated. Thus, ensure that you perform some research before you decide to work with a particular network or merchant. In this age of the internet, it is pretty easy to learn about businesses, thanks to review sites. If a merchant or an affiliate network scammed someone before, chances are the victim was so bitter and decided to alert other unsuspecting people through posting a negative review. You certainly want to stay away from a merchant or affiliate network that has earned plenty of negative reviews.

Use tools

We have made considerable advancements in technology. There are tools to help us execute various functions in almost every area of our life. When it comes to affiliate marketing, there are many tools both paid and free, that make our work easier. Ensure that you are using these tools in order to lighten your workload and increase your profits.

The Players Involved in Affiliate Marketing and Their Roles

One of the first things an individual must strive to understand as he or she thinks about getting into a field of business is the players in that particular business. This knowledge will help such an individual to have a better picture of the entire business process and to consider the best place to get in if indeed there are options for this. Knowing the different players, their roles, and possibly the amount of money each of them makes in comparison to the amount of time and effort they put in is perfect for setting goals as to where an individual would set his or her sights.

Therefore, an individual who is new to affiliate marketing must know the people or businesses he or she will be dealing with on a day-to-day basis, and what he or she will need to do to get paid. Some of the most successful affiliate marketers go even further to know the people they are competing with, in order for them to take advantage of current trends and look for ways to beat everyone else.

As mentioned before, Affiliate Marketing is a form of business where people, who in this case are the affiliates, earn an income by promoting products or services from other businesses and in the process; they earn a commission for their effort. In other words, affiliate marketers are like middlemen who never get to own the products they are selling.

Four core concepts lie at the heart of this form of online marketing. They include:

- Affiliate Marketing is performance-based – This is the main reason some people call it performance marketing. If a marketer does not perform, then he or she will not make any money
- The element of independence – This is the reason some people often refer to affiliates as independent marketers because they are free to handle their marketing campaigns in the best ways they can while setting their own rules
- The partnership element – This is what describes the collaborations and relationships between the key players involved. Every player needs to identify what his or her role is and know the rules governing how much money he or she will make after a sale goes through
- Universality - This means that the whole business works cross-channel

Main Players in Affiliate Marketing

There are several core players involved in Affiliate Marketing, and each plays a vital role in the process. They are:

- The merchant – advertiser, brand, or retailer
- The consumer
- The affiliate marketer is also called the publisher
- The affiliate network
- The affiliate program

However, the success of the entire process comes down to the relationship between the affiliate marketer and the merchant.

Merchant or Product Creator

The merchant or advertiser is the business whose products or services the affiliate marketer is promoting. It is quite easy for affiliates to find merchants and get them to work with them because it is a win-win situation for both players. Merchants are always ready to pay a commission for sales generated by affiliates because they would have had to pay even more money to their own full-time sales team. When affiliates fail to generate sales, merchants do not have to pay them. Therefore, it is cheaper and more convenient for them to use affiliate marketers. People can become merchants by doing the following:

- Coming up with a good product or service idea
- The building or creation of that product or service
- Getting affiliates to market their product or service

Affiliate Marketer

Affiliates are a vital component of the Affiliate Marketing scene, which is why it is called, well, Affiliate Marketing. They are the players who actually do the marketing. For example, a PC parts manufacturer may choose to work with affiliate marketers to increase its sales. In this case, the affiliates will set up blogs or websites about the PC parts and use innovative tools and techniques to promote the manufacturer's products. Therefore, when an individual goes online to look to buy a PC or find for a solution to his or her PC issues, he or she will read about it and learn what PC he or she needs to purchase or the parts to resolve the issue.

There are also several steps to becoming an affiliate, including:

- Finding the ideal and potentially profitable market niche – This is a very important step because the number of niches out there are too many to count
- Reviewing promising products and/or services in that niche – This will go a long way in encouraging the people who get to the affiliate's content to want to click on the link and hopefully make a purchase
- Building a website, blog, email list, and any other tool to reach the business's preferred audience – This is medium through which the affiliate marketer meets the people who can potentially click on their links, or where their visitors meet them
- Growing the business's audience using various marketing strategies

Affiliate Networks

Affiliate Marketing networks act as the meeting place for merchants and affiliates. It is where affiliates find and assess the different affiliates programs available and choose the ones that meet their needs. These networks are meant to make things easy for affiliates because they provide the information they need and help them pick the ideal program.

Affiliate Programs

Innovative brands usually run affiliate programs that allow affiliate marketers to sign up and work with them. These programs typically have everything worked out, including details of products and/or services which affiliates need to promote, as well as commissions payable and the method used to calculate them.

Affiliate programs make it easy for people who are new to Affiliate Marketing to acquire the vital information they need to succeed. However, there is a huge difference between good and bad performing programs. Amazon's associate's program is an example of an excellent affiliate program. Many affiliates are using it in their forums, websites, and blogs.

Consumer

Just like every other business, all efforts are geared towards making the consumer find value in whatever is on the market and facilitating the process to the point he or she pays for the goods or services. This individual purchases the merchant's products or services through an affiliate marketer. Sometimes, consumers may not even realize that they are part of a network. However, most affiliates choose to be upfront and transparent about their role because it can turn out to be in their own best interest. Some countries also require affiliates to disclose their association with the products they promote.

A Closer Look at the Affiliate Marketing System

The role people play in this system depends on their goals. Those who have a product or service to sell can become merchants and work with affiliates to market their products or services. On the other hand, those who want to simply market products and/or services and not have to deal with the physical or actual product or service should become affiliates. However, people can play both roles as well by selling their products or services through affiliates while promoting other people's products and services at the same time.

As more and more merchants jump into the bandwagon and start working with affiliate marketers, those that fail to leverage this opportunity are likely to lose their competitive edge. Affiliate Marketing is a great and profitable concept for all parties involved, including consumers who are able to learn more about the products and/or services they are interested in purchasing. Some marketing strategies applied by affiliates, such as coupons, are also beneficial to consumers.

Steps to Becoming an Affiliate Marketer

A quick Google search would have anyone who is not familiar with Affiliate Marketing believe that this business is about making tons of cash for doing nothing. The truth, however, is more complicated than that. Yes, some people have made a fortune through Affiliate Marketing over a ridiculously short period, but that is not everyone's story. It is also true that people can make money while they are sleeping at night or when they are away on holiday, but it does not mean that such individuals never work. Any level of success, especially in Affiliate Marketing, will require the laying down of a strong foundation, a lot of effort, and truckloads of patience.

On a basic level, Affiliate Marketing is a simple process consisting of three steps, namely:

- Recommending a product and/or service to the audience and visitors to a particular site
- Individuals in that audience buying the product or service using the provided affiliate link
- Earning a commission from the merchant for those purchases that were the result of an affiliate's marketing efforts

When it comes to becoming an affiliate marketer, an individual needs to build relationships with the consumers, merchants, and publishers.

Getting Started

Many prospective affiliates do not take the time to plan their moves carefully; instead, they simply join every affiliate program and network they come across. Consequently, they end up feeling overloaded and overwhelmed. People who want to succeed in this line of business should take their time and work through several important steps before they even attempt to promote a single product or service.

Find your Ideal Niche

Choosing a market niche will provide focus on an individual's business and help him or she creates solid and authoritative content. It will also simplify the process of coming up with targeted promotional campaigns. Some people consider this to be the most difficult part of starting an Affiliate Marketing business. Fortunately, there are ways to make it easier. They simply need to consider a few factors, including:

- What they are passionate about
- Whether their chosen topic is wide enough to create dozens of blog posts
- Whether the niche is overpopulated by other affiliates
- Whether there is money in that niche

These factors will help would-be affiliates determine whether it is worth investing time and effort into a particular niche or not.

Build a Website or Blog

Once they have picked a potentially lucrative niche, they are ready to create a blog or website. If they choose to start a blog, they need to choose the best blogging platform that will help them monetize their blog posts. Things to remember when creating a website or blog include:

- Make it personal
- Include contact information

- Insert a disclaimer if the blog or website is monetized
- Include a privacy policy
- Outline the terms of service
- Advertise to expand the audience who will become your clients
- Create Solid Content

In order to maximize on profits from Affiliate Marketing, an individual needs to create solid and compelling content which will whet the appetite of a visitor on his or her site and compel him or her to click on the link. He or she also needs to be knowledgeable in creating transactional and informational calls to action, as well as writing in a readable and interesting way. It is also important to make the content reader-focused by providing detailed information, answering reader questions, and writing in an engaging and accessible way. To accomplish this, knowledge of an affiliate marketer's audience is paramount.

Track Marketing Success

It is always important to know what works and what does not work. Therefore, new affiliate marketers should know how site visitors are engaging with their website. They can use a wide range of readily available analytics tools to get this information, which will help them make changes if needed.

Product or service Knowledge

Knowledge of the products and/or services you wish to sell will set the affiliate marketer apart from his or her competitors. Affiliate marketers make recommendations to their audiences of various products and/or services; therefore, they need to be knowledgeable in order to earn their audience's loyalty. Too often, however, new affiliates simply pick a few products they believe will be profitable without really getting to learn about them. More often than not, people will buy only after reading reviews from a site where the seller is giving them everything they need to know, including the things that are not so great. Therefore, if you will have to do a deep research of even have to purchase a product just to know how it feels, then you should go ahead.

Engage Site Visitors

Successful affiliate marketers understand the importance of engaging with their audiences. For example, those who have a blog will often provide a way through which readers can leave comments. Interacting with site visitors offers affiliates the opportunity to have conversations with the people they hope will use their links to make a purchase. Essentially, engaging site visitors will make them come to consider that your site is a place where like-minded people can meet, which will lead to more conversions to your advantage.

Focus on Providing Information

Self-promotion and blatant sales sites rarely gain traction, because most people often feel as if it is annoying and disturbing. In order to grow their audience, affiliate marketers should concentrate on offering relevant information and helping their audience get the answers to questions they might have. Therefore, it is important to conduct research and offer a more updated and detailed product or service information in comparison to your competition.

Always Test and Improve

Affiliates should always strive to improve their marketing process. Like any other learning process, Affiliate Marketing is an ongoing endeavor. Affiliates need to learn and improve as they go, including dedicating adequate time for improvement.

A new affiliate marketer will not make a fortune within a month. Therefore, it is important to set proper expectations in order to handle the normal ups and downs of business. The right goals and expectations will help them work patiently towards meeting them. The steps outlined above, however, can go a long way into helping anyone become a successful affiliate marketer.

How Affiliate Marketers Get Paid

Merchants looking to find a cost-effective way to generate sales should take a closer look at Affiliate Marketing. Since a third party receives the sales or leads information of each affiliate, it only pays based on the results of the goals they have set in their agreements. The pay may be the result of an actual sale, a lead, or a sign of interest.

When choosing a goal to set and the payment method, the needs of both the affiliate and the merchant should be carefully considered. The merchant needs to think about the cost per sale to ensure he or she is spending within his or her margins. The affiliate, on the other hand, needs to choose a payment model that will earn him or her the highest possible revenue for the traffic he or she sends to the merchant's website. The secret to choosing the best model for both parties is finding the right balance.

The payment model for Affiliate Marketing is one of the most important factors affiliates need to sort out prior to launching their marketing campaigns.

In addition to the payment models, affiliates need to think about the following:

- Payouts – What percentage of the total sale will they get
- Reversals and locking periods – How will the parties deal with reversals and how long are the locking periods
- Incentives – What incentives are available for the marketer, just to keep him or her selling all day and night
- Frequency – How many times will an affiliate expect to receive payment over a specified period

Payment thresholds – How much money should an affiliate marketer have to make before withdrawing his or her earnings and what is the limit of interest payable for a particular product or service

Choosing Affiliate Marketing Payment Models

Most affiliates choose their model based on its range of verticals, offers, perks, and so on. However, many of them feel like they cannot rely on any method to receive their hard-earned cash. In fact, some of them have stopped working with their particular network because of a payment dispute. Therefore, affiliates should consider certain important factors when choosing a payment system, including:

- Reasonable commission feel
- The time it takes to receive payment
- Payment system accessibility
- An easy, clear, and fast verification process
- Common Affiliate Payment Models
- PPS – Pay per Sale

This is one of the most popular and least risky payment models. In fact, the affiliate business was built on this model. In this instance, affiliates receive payment following a completed sale. If the affiliate fails to drive a sale, the merchant has no obligation to pay him or her. This payment method encourages affiliates to push harder and seek maximum exposure to secure more conversions.

The level of commission for PPS varies according to the merchant involved. Some merchants operating through affiliate networks will compete against each other for the best affiliate marketers through different rates of PPS. Large brands, however, usually pay a lower rate of PPS.

PPL – Pay per Lead

Sometimes, affiliate-driven action is about more than sales alone. Newsletter subscriptions and free trials may be valuable to merchants as well since they can help turn potential consumers into paying consumers. Merchants offering these programs reward their affiliates based on the number of people they refer who subscribe as leads. Essentially, these people provide some requested information, which can be used by the merchant as a sales lead.

PPC – Pay per Call

This payment model is ideal for service merchants, from law firms and estate agents to financial consultants and home-renovation contractors. It is also used by merchants who sell luxury goods, such as expensive watches, diamonds, and luxury cruises. Affiliate marketers earn a fee based on the number of people they convince to call the particular merchant offering this type of program.

PPC – Pay per Click

In this model, affiliates earn a fee based on the number of visitors who click on their affiliate links to go to the merchant's website. These visitors do not have to buy anything from the merchant, also, it does not matter to the affiliates what they do once they get to the merchant's website. All that matters to affiliates using this payment model is for visitors to click on their links.

Combined Payment Models

In order to attract the best affiliates and maximize affiliate sales, many merchants choose to offer more than one type of payment model. A combined payment model is also profitable to affiliates, as it allows them to earn a reward for leads as well as qualifying purchases.

Affiliate Incentives

In order for affiliates to promote a company's products and services actively, they need to be fairly rewarded for their time and effort. They also need to be motivated to do better, which is where incentives come in. Incentive offers are entirely up to the merchant. They can choose to offer only one incentive or a combination of two or three incentives. These incentives include:

- Commission increases
- Prizes
- Cash bonuses

These incentives can be offered to affiliates who meet certain conditions, or the first affiliate who does. In addition, there are a number of pay per impression payment systems, such as pay-per-view, that reward affiliates based on the number of people who view their advertisements.

The advantage that Affiliate Marketing has over traditional marketing is that it is an affiliate system. Essentially, merchants only reward their affiliates when they achieve the desired result. Traditional advertising, on the other hand, is more risky for merchants because they end up spending money on advertising based on an estimation of its effectiveness.

Reasons Why You Need a Website

Surprisingly, many people still do not understand the power of a website and the benefits it can provide their businesses, which is why they lack an online presence in this day and age. If you run a business but lack a website, you are probably losing out on tons of opportunities for your business. Websites are not only for people who make money solely online, such as affiliate marketers. Rather, any type of business can use them to accomplish different objectives aimed at maximizing revenues and business growth.

Today, there are many online avenues, which businesses can use to make their presence known, for example, social media. However, the profit potential of a running website should not be underestimated. Many online entrepreneurs have started small and made a fortune through their websites. Affiliate Marketing websites such as skyscanner.com, makingsenseofcents.com, and moneysavingexpert.com are great examples of successful websites that have made bank for their owners.

Chapter 2. Keyword Research

The quality guidelines are then presented. Web administrators must adhere to these in order to benefit from a sustainable ranking. The next step is a detailed presentation of the necessary changes to a website, which increase the ranking many times over. These are on-page SEO measures. According to these informative instructions, the structured data are happy about an extensive dedication, as they also improve the ranking of a website. Beyond that the OFF-Page SEO is explained in detail, because this is not to be excluded from a successful search machine optimization no more.

Keyword research

Keyword research is an elementary function in search engine optimization. Without this activity the success of a website is definitely doomed to failure. Keywords are keywords with which both webmasters and users associate an Internet presence. These must therefore be chosen with care. Furthermore, web designers slip into the role of their website visitors during keyword research. They locate phrases and keywords that users enter in search engines. Then they place them in a clever way in their online presence in order to appear as high as possible in the organic (unpaid) search results. The challenge, however, is to find the right keywords that are popular with users but stand out from the competition.

Types of keywords

There are different types of keywords. With regard to the intention of the users, keywords can be divided into three different groups. These consist of commercial, informative and navigating keywords.

Commercial keywords enter the users who have a purchase intention. A classic example of this would be "Buying a Travel Guide to the USA". Those who sell the product they are looking for should choose their keywords carefully and always be careful to signal the intention to buy.

When choosing the keywords "Travel Tips USA", however, users who enter these terms have the intention of receiving free travel tips. Thus, the main intention of this user is definitely not to visit a paid travel guide. However, providers who offer an article with free travel tips for the USA and want to advertise their travel guide at the end of the text can use this keyword. Users searching for information on a specific topic use informative keywords. The question: "How big is the Eiffel Tower?" is a classic example of the use of informative keywords. Such questions are also ideal for Voice SEO. Webmasters who use these keywords will definitely not find any users who have a purchase intention.

Short or head tail keywords consist of only one term. Even though this keyword species is a non-specific genus, it covers a huge spectrum. Mid tail key words mainly contain two to three terms and represent the middle of the extremely unspecific short tail and specific long tail keywords.

Long tail keywords usually contain more than four terms. This keyword is a specific type of keyword that becomes more and more exact thanks to the addition of additional terms.

An example of a short or head tail keyword would be the term "bread". The mid tail keyword extension could be "bake bread". The final long tail keyword might be "bake bread at home".

Finding the right keywords for successful search engine optimization

The keyword research of search engine optimization stands for the search for a suitable keyword to a website. Users use the selected keyword to locate the particular page on the Internet. Accordingly, the choice of the keyword plays the leading role. However, this should not only match the website content, but should also be searched for by the selected target group. However, the term keyword does not only stand for a single keyword, but also defines a text unit that can either be found in the text or briefly represents the content of the text as a suitable keyword. Accordingly, keywords are created from several terms and numbers. They are representatives for terms, about which a text is found at best with Google as well as further search engines. The biggest challenge for webmasters lies in their ability to put themselves in their target group. In practice, it often happens that websites are optimized for unsuitable keywords because the target group uses completely different names than the website operator. The aim of keyword research is to find the words that the majority of the target group members are looking for.

The distinction between good and bad keywords

Before the instructions for a successful keyword search are dealt with, the distinction between good and bad keywords is made.

An online retailer who sells outerwear such as T-shirts, jackets or pullovers would probably at first glance choose the keyword "outerwear", which is theoretically perfectly correct, but in practice less well received by the searcher. The question is whether the target group is actually looking for "outerwear". The answer is rather no. The keyword "outerwear" is a Head Tail Keyword, which is not commercial. Even if it could achieve a high search volume, the number of connections would be extremely low because this keyword is too inaccurate. The keywords "T-shirt" or "jacket" do not represent a suitable alternative either, because they do not indicate which target the searchers are aiming for, because they are not a commercial keyword. If the individuals want to make a purchase, they will rather enter the keywords "buy jacket" (commercial keyword). Online merchants who only rank their shop for the term "jacket" by no means address their desired target group directly. The keyword research thus aims at a precise formulation and exact alignment of the keywords.

In general, the principle applies: "The more general a keyword is, the greater the number of suitable pages Google will find". At the same time, this leads to enormous competition. As a result, the online retailer's chance of getting to the first page, who only ranked his shop after the keyword "jacket", drops considerably. Therefore a keyword, which describes the respective offer of the side as exactly as possible, should be the main goal. However, it should be a commercial keyword. In this way, entrepreneurs reach their target group with significantly less effort.

Recommendation of keyword species

In order to find suitable keywords, the knowledge of the correct keyword type is absolutely necessary. At times, long tail keywords dominated search engine optimization. This is partly due to the small number of competitors. That is why website operators can quickly move up to the top rank of search queries. However, the problem with long tail keywords lies in their search volume. A search volume of 100 is not enough to be successful with a website. For this reason, an optimization of similar long tail keywords and related texts takes place using different keywords. Therefore it is not recommended that a page presents five individual web pages with the same topic but optimized with different long tail keywords. This increases the search volume. However, this strategy has had its day. Google is now extremely clever and recognizes these tricks. This strategy came to an end at the latest with the so-called Panda Update. For this reason, website operators rank only as a single long tail keyword, which however reduces the search volume. The following overview summarizes the disadvantages of long tail keywords.

Latest updates prevent Google ranking of different pages on the same topic.

The search volume is extremely small.

Contributions of inferior quality have a negative impact on the authority of the website.

Due to the mentioned disadvantages it is worthwhile to switch to Mid Tail Keywords. Even if these are highly competitive, with a good choice and consistent content promotion, they can quickly catapult a website into the top ranks.

However, the competition is the greatest with short tail keywords. But webmasters reach the largest number of users with this keyword type. However, practice has proven that short tail keywords are not the right choice. Therefore Mid Tail Keywords are best suited. Their competition is limited. This is partly because they are not as general as short tail keywords. In addition, they increase the probability of a financial statement.

A carefully conducted keyword research saves the webmasters not only time, but also money. A suitable keyword is the prerequisite for earning money. Unsuitable keywords that do not match the website content do not provide added value for the searcher. In addition, careful webmasters with a good keyword research can find keywords that competitors do not use. In this way, webmasters benefit from the comparative competitive advantages. Suitable methods and structured procedures for keyword research

The following keyword search can be done with Google. Webmasters do not need any tools with costs for this manual. Accordingly, the displayed keyword research is free of charge.

Keyword brainstorming

Write down keywords that match the website in question

The keyword is surrounded by a cloud with matching additional terms

If the example keyword is "baking bread", other terms such as gluten-free, whole meal flour, sunflower bread or baguette can surround the main keyword.

In order to be able to better understand and apply these measures, the techniques described are carried out using the keyword "baking bread" as an example.

Keyword Input into a suitable keyword tool

The following instructions are for a successful keyword search, which is carried out with Google. The Google Keyword Planner can help. Webmasters can also use other keyword tools, which they can use for free. After the tool has been selected, the keyword is entered into the selected tool. Those who want to do the keyword research with AdWords only need a Google account. The webmasters then simply enter their main term in the Keyword Planner Tool under "Search for new keywords using a phrase, a web page and a category". When you click on Ideas Retrieve, different ones are displayed.

Sorting the list in keyword search according to the respective search volume

As a result, users receive a whole list of keyword suggestions that correspond to the main term. With a click on the field called "Average search queries per month" webmasters can arrange them from large to small. The keywords that stand out due to the highest search volume appear in the upper rank. At the end or on the last result pages of this list, keywords with a small search volume are mentioned. Usually these are long tail keywords. The middle ranks are important for webmasters, as the majority of mid tail keywords are placed here. Based on this ad, website operators select a keyword that best matches the content of their online presence. It is advisable to take a look at the column called "Competition" and also to inspect the climbing pages for the respective mid tail keyword. However, since the Google Keyword Planner is an AdWords tool, the competition does not refer to the display of search results, but to general ads. For this reason, webmasters may not neglect the climbing web pages to the respective keyword.

Competitive intelligence

At this step, webmasters analyze their competitors to a keyword. There are different indicators for this. The competition can serve both as an indication of how powerful the competition is and the "interrupted bid". The higher the bid, the higher the competition. However, website designers do not rely solely on this information. This is because a certain keyword is extremely expensive to display and enjoys great popularity, but is not very successful in organic search results. In order to find out how big the competition for the selected keyword is, it is worth applying the following techniques.

Enter the URL, the domain metrics, and a check of the backlinks.

Control of ON-Page Optimization

Check the respective search results on question-answer pages or in forums

Inspect content quality more closely

In order to better understand and apply these measures, the techniques described are carried out using the example keyword "baking bread".

Input of the URL, the domain metrics as well as a check of the backlinks

In this step, webmasters use a tool that presents them with important metrics. The free tool called "SEO Toolbar" of the developer named MOZ can be helpful. It requires an installation. After the successful setup of the toolbar, the keyword input takes place at Google. Among the current results, the toolbar with all the metrics for the matching page and domain now appears without further ado. Webmasters are particularly interested in the values URL Rating, Backlinks / Linking Domains to the Website, Domain Rating and Backlinks / Linking Domains to the Complete Page. The first step is an analysis of the URL rating. This represents the strength of a single page. In this case, the majority of the values are below 20. Ultimately, this means that competition is more in the lower range. Webmasters should not miss the information on how this website is linked. For this reason, naming the source of the back link is indispensable. To fulfill this task, you need a so-called Back Link Checker. Those who do not have a tool that can display backlinks to a domain can choose a free tool. When analyzing the back link of a page that is ranked first, experts advise you to consider the following aspects. Based on the domain rating, webmasters read that strong domains link to this page. As a rule, these are topic-relevant websites. For example, the link type overview shows that of the 41 backlinks, only one is marked "NoFollow". Therefore almost all backlinks are of high quality. Google attaches great importance to the content presented. The site, which has taken first place, offers users an informative contribution in which they can also find general information on the subject of "baking bread". Finally, the metrics for the respective domains are analyzed. If almost all of them have a domain rating of over 50 and only thousands or even several million backlinks, webmasters should realize that they can only compete with other websites with difficulty on this keyword.

Control of OnPage Optimization

Since ON-Page Optimization is an important aspect of search engine optimization, many pages that have not been optimized point to low competition. With the ON-Page Optimization Control, webmasters take a closer look at the search results. You check whether the selected keyword is present in the title tags. Almost all entries use the keyword "buy food supplements". In

order to get to the bottom of this fact, webmasters should nevertheless take a closer look at the individual pages. Important hints for optimization are provided, for example:
- Keywordplacement in H1 + H2 headings.
- Keyword placement in the respective URL
Web designers have the option to view the website and manually perform the ON-Page Optimization check or use OneProSEO's free SEO Check Tool. This performs the control of the ON-Page optimization. If the keyword should appear in the URL as well as in the numerous H1 headings, except in the H2 headings, this does not mean that the page was optimized badly. Webmasters should take this step to control the first top ten websites. If they find one or two pages that have not been optimized, they can consider this indication as an indicator of a keyword with little competition.

Check the respective search results on question-answer pages or in forums. For some keywords, questions from question-answer pages or forums such as "gutefrage.net" can also appear in the Top 10. This notice proves how inadequately the competitors' site has been optimized in relation to this keyword.

Inspect content quality more closely.

The step of controlling content quality is the most important aspect of keyword research. Webmasters take a close look at the contents of the individual pages. If they find predominantly modest information or boring and much too short articles on the subject of "buying dietary supplements", this provides a clear indication of weak competition. However, if the articles on this topic are exclusively long and informative, then it is definitely a strong keyword. For this reason, it is worth searching for an alternative keyword. The already mentioned profile can serve as an important aid.

The keyword planner from Google

People searching for a keyword in Google's Keyword Planner now find the exact number of keywords and the corresponding search volume in the relevant column. Google's Keyword Planner allows its users to continue to check the exact search volume. But for that they have to accept some obstacles.

In the first step webmasters select the function "Determine new keywords". They then perform an ordinary search for a keyword.

After that, webmasters should make sure that they have selected the target region Germany. The default setting always refers to the USA. Therefore, it is important to observe this setting. After clicking on the target region and the corresponding language, users can enjoy a German version.

The keyword planner now displays a list with the search volume and the search term. It provides meaningful ideas for keywords that webmasters can use. In addition, the users receive information regarding keywords of the advertisements of their competitors. However, they should not adopt them one-to-one under any circumstances. A detailed explanation in this regard follows on the following pages.

Use Wikipedia as a template for suitable keywords

Not only forums, but also Wikipedia can support webmasters with keyword research. In this huge online encyclopedia, numerous people make the daily effort to classify contributions to different terms into suitable categories. All webmasters need to do is call up the "wikpedia.de" website and enter the keyword they would like to search for in the search bar at the top right. For search engine optimization, the table of contents is particularly interesting because it can provide crucial ideas.

Related searches from Google

Webmasters can, for example, enter the term "search engine optimization" in Google and scroll to the bottom of the page. There you will see the "relatives search queries". Thanks to this function, motivated website designers can quickly and easily find mid tail keywords that are directly linked to a large short tail keyword and could therefore be great as their main keyword.

Chapter 3. Social Media & SEO

Dominating social media in actuality is going to require you to focus your social media platform with a clear approach, defined goals, and a strategy that will help you reach those goals. Creating a multi-platform approach requires you to know how to leverage each platform, how you can build a massive following on each platform, and then how to turn that platform into a working social media sales funnel. Before you can start creating your strategy and determining how to grow on each platform, you need to decide what your goals are and how you can best reach those goals using social media. Each platform is going to provide you with slightly different benefits. So, by identifying your goals first, you can ensure that you are going to be using the right platforms and enforcing the right strategies to maximize your time investment on social media.

Creating Your Business Goals

The first thing you want to do is create your business goals for these year. Typically, all of your other strategic goals should directly reflect your overall business goals. By knowing exactly what it is that you are trying to accomplish in your business in the immediate future, you can start creating goals for your social media platforms as well. You can set one or more goals for your business in the near future, though you should be intentional about setting only one or two goals as your primary focus for the year. This way, you are clear on exactly what it is that you are working toward and you can design every secondary goal and strategy around that primary goal in your business.

The best way to create your business goal is to look at what means the most to you and your business for the coming year and create your goals around that concept. If you are brand new in business, you might set the goal to make your first year profitable in business. Identify what exact number that would be for you. Or, you might set the goal to increase your brand awareness and start connecting with a broader audience so that you have a system of trusted people to invest in your business as you continue to grow your brand name and popularity over the years to come. If you have been in business longer, your goal may be to refocus your brand on something slightly different and bring your audience along on that adjustment with you. You might try to increase your profits this year so that you can hire more employees or offer more to your audience.

Whatever your goals may be, make sure that you use the S.M.A.R.T planning goal style to ensure that you are setting goals that you can actually achieve this same year. So, your goals need to be specific, measurable, attainable, realistic, and timely. For example, rather than saying "I want to earn a six-figure year in these year" you could say "I want to earn $125,000 in revenue by December 31, of these year through my business." When you set specific goals, it becomes easier for you to know whether or not you are effectively moving toward your goals. This way you can determine if your strategies are working or if they need to be adjusted to help you advance more effectively.

Creating Your Social Media Goals

Once you have your general business goals created, you can start determining what your social media goals are going to be. It is important to realize that social media works differently for different business models. Approaching your social media goals requires you to consider what exactly social media can do for you and how you can maintain your image while incorporating social media into your strategy. For example, if you are a lawyer, you may not want to use social media as openly as another business because you cannot freely share certain information. In certain industries, you will need to be more conservative in your approach, which means that your goals should reflect these conservative social media values. So, if you were a lawyer on Instagram, rather than being open and sharing snippets of your life online, you would likely refrain from using stories or IGTV altogether and instead simply create posts on your feed. These posts should be targeted specifically toward your desired audience by providing them with the information that they need to know, then direct them to your website or your phone number so that you can talk privately with them. In this scenario, your social media goals would be to entirely get people to contact you, rather than to build a massive following and become a well-liked influencer in your industry.

You can determine which style of social media goals you need quite simply. If you run a more professional business where you need to keep a large portion of information private, then you need to use social media to drive people to contact you. If you run a brick and mortar store, then you need to use social media to drive people into your store so that they can shop with you. If you run an online business, then you need to build your following so that you can market to a larger audience.

That being said, you still need to be more specific when you are setting social media goals. What exactly are you trying to achieve through social media? For example, if you are the owner of a coffee shop, do you want to drive more tourists to your coffee shop so that they can take pictures with your photo ops and increase the popularity of your shop? Or, do you want to increase the amount of local individuals who are coming through your doors to purchase coffee and become loyal visitors? If you are an influencer, maybe you want to increase your following so that you can generate pitches for popular brands and start earning more income through your platform.

Whatever it is that you desire to do, make sure that you are utilizing social media as a tool in your overall goals and not relying on it as the exclusive strategy itself. Even if social media is your primary method for reaching out to your audience, you should recognize that your business itself is not exclusive to social media. You will still have plenty of other things that need to happen in order for you to achieve your goals. When you see social media as a tool and organize it into your overall strategy as a tool, you put yourself in the position where you can start using social media as one of your most powerful forces online.

Determining What Platforms Will Work Best for You

After determining what your goals are for social media, you have one last thing that you need to consider before beginning the process of designing your social media strategy. You need to determine what platforms are going to be the most effective for you when it comes to achieving the goals that you have set out to achieve. In each of the following sections, you are going to learn about the six biggest social media platforms that presently exist, how they can be used, and who will most benefit from them. Make sure that you read through this information and choose platforms that are actually going to support you in achieving your goals so that you are focusing your efforts in areas that make sense to your overall goals and business.

Understanding SEO

Search Engine Optimization (SEO) is increasingly becoming a more integral part of any business's marketing strategy as easy visibility from a basic Google or Bing search remains the simplest and most effective way to draw in new customers. SEO can be difficult for those running a small business to begin using without some prior training as there are several different facets required to use them effectively. For example, SEO is just as much about what content you use to populate your site as it is about the way your entire website is structured.

While other means, including having an active social media presence, will help to generate some additional traffic for your site, they are much more effective when used as a way that maximizes SEO at the same time. As such, it is important to take the time to ensure that the content from your website, as well as the website itself, is as readily available to the relevant databases as possible. While this process may seem difficult and time consuming at first, the results will always far outweigh the costs. What's more, improving your SEO is free marketing, not committing to it fully is akin to leaving money on the table.

Search engines such as Bing or Google work by sending out automated programs known as crawlers to follow the links to various URLs for every website that is currently online. The crawlers then track relevant data from each page before sending that information to databases which compile it before sending the results to users when queried. Due to the amount of data being parsed, keywords were originally used to make things easier to handle.

As knowledge and understanding of how to game the system grew, simple keywords were no longer enough and now there are a wide variety of different factors including popularity, backlinks, descriptions and more that help users to return reliable results in seconds. This is what makes SEO so crucial as not succeeding in all areas can often be akin to not succeeding at all as your site will be passed over by sites who are firing on all cylinders.

This is why common terms that potential users might employ carry such weight as targeting the right type of search engine traffic can be the difference between success and failure for your fledgling affiliate marketing business. What's worse, filling in the right boxes with wrong details can burry your completely competent site under inferior results to ensure that practically no one will ever be able to find it.

While SEO is a hotly debated subject, the good news is that you can get by without hiring an expert if you are willing to do the leg work yourself and keep up with it in the long-term. While this won't have you leading the pack, it will at least keep you in the running. When it comes to getting started improving your SEO by yourself, the biggest cost is going to come in terms of the time commitment that you put forth in improving your website's SEO. The following tips will help you get started on the right foot.

Choosing keywords

When it comes to choosing the best keywords for your website, your first thoughts are going to be words that will see the greatest number of hits overall. Truly successful keywords go beyond this, however, and reflect how a website or company pictures itself at a fundamental level.

Focus on key phrases: In hopes of finding more useful details, keywords have grown into key phrases over the years and finding the right one for you is crucial to your long-term success. While it can be easy to overthink the process, the goal should be to find something that isn't too broad to be useful or too narrow to generate reasonable results. For example, if your website sells nutritionally conscious dog food, then on their own the words food and dog will not get you where you need to be. Instead, a better choice would be to choose words that relate to the specialty ingredients your dog foods contain.

Ideally, you are going to want to choose key phrases that are between 2 and 4 words that relate to your website in the most general terms possible. This means it is best to do some additional research up front as you may be surprised to find some common phrases are actually quite unpopular for whatever reason. The fewer search results you return when testing out these words, the less popular the phrase is with the public. Again, your goal should be able to find key phrases that are popular enough to see use without generating so many hits that it is completely ineffective.

Don't think of them as a contest: While it can be tempting to go at top search results by trying to compete for the same keywords directly, this is rarely going to work in your favor. As the new website on the totem pole, your results are automatically going to be lower than a website that has had time to establish itself in the market. Rather than going to the king directly, instead, try developing your own following around a related keyword before dipping your toes in the more competitive space.

While finding yourself at the top of that particular search can provide an ego boost, the odds of it happening are rarely in favor of anyone other than major corporations or sites that include the keyword in their name. It is therefore almost always better to go with something more precisely tailored to your business while still being a reasonable thing for someone to type into a search engine.

Pop some tags

Metadata tags are similar to keywords and key phrases in that they make it more likely that your pages ae going to show up within relevant search results. Unlike with keywords, however, they do not typically show up on the pages themselves and are typically only visible within the code of the pages in question. You can think of metadata tags as the keywords of the underlying data. Meta data tags can be viewed on any page by simply right-clicking on it and then selecting the option to view page source. The meta tag specifics will be found near the top of the screen. Meta tags can be altered by anyone with a basic understanding of HTML, or, from the appropriate menu option from the backend of your website.

There are four primary types of meta tags that you are going to want to use when it comes to trying to improve your SEO, meta attribute keywords are those that are related to the current page specifically, the title tag is the name that the search engine displays when the page is referenced and the meta attribute description is the description that comes up as part of the search result. Finally, the robots meta attribute is used to ensure that crawlers know to document the page.

Due to the glut of keyword stuffing over the past decade, the keyword attribute has decreased in value when compared to the other attributes, nevertheless, it will still give you a small SEO bump when compared to those websites that don't use it at all. The most important meta tag these days is the title tag which is why it is important to always take the time to ensure that it is formatted properly on each and every one of your pages. It is important to choose a title tag that clearly indicates what the content in question contains while also including at least one key phrase if at all possible. Remember, the title is what is going to show up in all of your search results, so it is important that it is a good one.

If you manage to make it to the top page of Google results but you aren't at the top of the top, then it is going to most likely be the description attribute that pushes you over the edge. You have 20 words to sway potential visitors to your site that your link is going to provide them with the details they need, while also telling Google how to classify your page. Take some time to think about it and make those 20 words as impactful as possible.

If you aren't sure where to start, a good place is by trying to include as many relevant key phrases into this section as you can manage. While their use here won't directly improve your SEO, studies show that seeing the words they are looking for in a description makes potential viewers more likely to choose one search result over another. Just make sure you do more than list a bunch of keywords, a legible sentence of text is key to proving your site is full of viable content as well.

Robot Attribute: The robot attribute is perhaps the most straightforward of all of the modifiable attributes as there are only two options you can choose from. The index/noindex option tells various search engines whether or not you want your page to be returned from basic search results. The follow/nofollow option, on the other hand, tells crawlers whether or not they are supposed to follow links on your pages to their destinations or not. In most instances, you should choose index and follow respectively.

Chapter 4.   How to find A Niche

We are going to assume that you will be using a blog to market your products as many affiliates do. This is why we will not give you some great insights on how to market, but it will also help you get more sales. If you don't pick the right niche, well then god help you. If you pick out the wrong niche for your blog, then you might as well say goodbye to your dreams of becoming a full-time blogger.

When it comes to picking out the right niche for your blog, there are many things to consider before you pick the right topic. It would be best if you made sure that the topic you decide to write on isn't too saturated, meaning that there aren't many bloggers already writing about it.

On the contrary, you do not want a topic which is "super-niche" meaning that it would be hard for someone to drive traffic to the website. Lastly, it would help if you made sure that there are great affiliate options for the niche. Granted most niches have affiliate options but are they going to make money that's another question to consider.

Moreover, give you some tools on how to find a topic to write on which is already getting the right amount of traffic for you to start earning some money.

Pick a niche you enjoy

If you are not having fun with what you are writing about, then chances are you won't make a dime from it. People are brilliant at sniffing out someone who is not involved in the topic, so it is a must that whichever niche you decide to start your blog on, it needs to be something you are interested in or at least remotely interested in.

The best way to find out your niche would be to ask yourself what your interests are and hobbies if you love yoga and if you do yoga regularly, then that could be an option for you. Ask yourself what your hobbies or passion are, everybody has a passion or hobby they enjoy. I am quite sure that you do as well, so find it and write it.

Micro-niche

Once you have decided on a topic to write on, it would be time to find out the competition there is. To find out, search up your niche on google and look for the "About" right underneath the search engine.

You will see a number which is most likely in the millions, and you want to be looking at a number which is less than 50 million and above 1 million for it to be in the "sweet spot" for picking out the right niche. Anything more than 50 million would equal high saturation, and less than 1 million would mean there is a lesser chance of you making it profitable.

Affiliate marketing

We will discuss affiliate marketing further, but it is crucial that you do some research and find out your opportunities in your selected niche before you start up your blog. For readers that have no idea as to what affiliate marketing is, it is where you have a product on your blog with a unique link only unique to your website. Whenever someone decides to buy that specific product from your link, you will get a commission.

Affiliate marketing is how most if not all bloggers earn their money, so do not overlook this step. The best way to find out if your topic has the right affiliate programs is for you should go on Amazon.com and check out all the products for sale related to your niche, if they have a lot of products available for you to market then you have found the one. We will discuss more options regarding affiliate marketing, but for now, worry about Amazon and the products they have to offer.

Monetizing

Monetizing your blog means that you will allow Google to run ads on your blog, and whenever they click onto that ad you will get paid. The best way to find out if your niche is getting a lot of Google advertising, just google your "keyword."

If your topic is yoga, google yoga in the search bar, the more ads you see related to your niche the better chances you have of making money from monetizing your blog. Monetizing is a great way to make some more money from your blog, especially if you have many visitors to your blog.

Final research

Now to seal the deal with your topic, you need to go onto "Google trends." This is where you will find out how consistent your topic is, and how many people are actively looking for articles on your niche. All you have to do is type in your keyword into the search engine, and it will present you with a graph.

Make sure you are looking at a graph with at least five years of data, now if your diagram is in the middle to high mark while staying consistent at the same time then you have picked out the right topic. Whereas if your graph is slowly declining year by year, then it is time for you to find a new blog topic.

If all these criteria check out, then you have the right niche and you can start up your blog right away. If that's not the case, then I want you to reevaluate your topics and come up with a new one that does meet all the criteria listed above.

After all, you need to make sure that you are making money from your blog and not just writing for the sake of it. Keep searching and keep looking, and you will find your golden topic. Trust me you should be able to find your topic within a couple of tries.

How to write your blog to sell?

It is time for you to write your very first blog post, you might be very excited or super nervous. Either way, your first post is not going to be the best. However, don't let that stop you from writing one as I want you to try your best and post one. You will learn and grow with your blog and writing, but don't expect perfection from the get-go. As it takes time and practical lessons before you become a professional blogger so to speak.

Remember as long as you have decent writing skills, meaning that you can write a sentence and you have some knowledge on the topic at hand then you should be ok. If you have been doing your research online, then you might have read about a million ways to write a blog post. For the sake of this book, we will make a dummy-proof system that can be used for anyone to write up a great article. We will be utilizing a method known as the P.A.S method, which is simple to use and has been used by many bloggers with great success.

The best part about this method is you can write a typical blog post with no affiliate links, and you can also use it for selling products through your affiliate link. With that note, we will talk about P: problem A: agitate S: solve method in more depth. We will also write up an example article of the PAS method for the readers to understand it better.

P: problem

Just like the title says it is a problem, I want you to understand your niche and the readers it brings. If your blog is about how to lose body fat and stay healthy, then I want you to start the article by displaying the problems to the readers. The way to do it is by making it relatable, make the readers feel like you know their struggles and pain. Bring it out in the first section of the article.

A: agitate

In the second section of the blog, I want to further the pain. You have managed to find the pain point of your readers, and now you need to make it more emotionally connecting to the readers. Make the readers feel like they need to find a solution to their problem, as soon as possible because they can't live like this. Also, don't talk about the issues too much as it will make you sound weak and not helpful.

S: solve

Now finally, you will be offering the readers a way out of their problem! You are their savior. This could be either an affiliate link to a product that will solve their solution or, it can be a solution you could offer your readers to gain trust. Don't keep sending them to affiliate links all the time, as this will look like you are trying to make a buck from them and not help. Use a method known as the "jab, jab, jab, hook," You write three articles free of knowledge and the fourth one is where you add an affiliate link.

P.A.S (in action)

You might have read online how you can lose 50 lbs. in 4 months by taking this magic pill or following a $1,000 workout program, let me save you some time and let you in on a little secret NONE of this work. I have been where you are right now, struggling to lose weight and can't seem to find a way out.

I know that you have tried and failed a thousand times, and you still can't seem to achieve the results you have been striving for. I can understand it is hard, you try and find a plan for success, but you end up getting disappointed.

Truthfully we both know you cannot live like this, there are a lot more things to enjoy in life which you haven't experienced because you are overweight. I can say that because I have been there, I use to be 50 lbs. overweight trying to lose it. After trying everything, I managed to find a way out of this mess.

Which was using this plan known as "get fit." I lost 50 lbs. in a matter of 4 months, and I haven't looked back since then. I can finally move more freely and experience more things in life. If you are struggling to lose your weight like I was, then clicking the link below will take you to a page with a discount code where you can get a copy of yourself. I can't wait to see you live a healthy life like I am!

If you read the example article carefully, then you can see how I have managed to implement all three methods in the P.A.S smoothly. That should be your goal when you are writing up your article, make it flow. My recommendation would be to write your first three articles without any affiliate links, help your new readers for free so they can gain trust in you.

Once you do decide to add an affiliate link of yours, then the chances of them converting would be higher compared to if you didn't provide them with free information. Also, don't worry about writing your articles in many different ways. You can quickly scale up your blog to $3,000 a month by only using the P.A.S method.

Furthermore, don't forget to add a featured image to your blog post. You can find HD images for free at many free websites, make sure the pictures are HD and are related to your blog post.

Just remember not to chase perfection as it will lead you disappointed, instead try your best and show it to the world. You will learn a lot more from practical experiences rather than trying to read this book and making it perfect, use this book as a guide and embark on your own journey.

Chapter 5. How to Structure Your Site for Easy and Automatic SEO

Once you have taken the time to find a niche that you know people are going to want to be a part of, the next step will be to set up a website that provides you with everything you need to get started creating the type of content that people are going to want to see.

Start with a WordPress site: While, if you have never built a website, you may not personally be familiar with WordPress, you have without a doubt used a WordPress site or 2 at one time or another, likely in the past 72 hours. There are more than 25 million currently active WordPress websites which makes it the most widely used platform worldwide by a fair margin and it counts major brands like Pepsi, Ford and Samsung among its users. What's more, you can get started for free to ensure that you like it before you have to commit to anything in the long term.

While there are plenty of alternatives out there, WordPress has been used to create more than one billion websites for a reason, starting with the fact that you can get started for free before converting to a paid service once you actually see some money start coming in. What's more, if you can use a word processor then you can use WordPress's interface to add new content to your site with just a few clicks. What's also nice is that each new piece of content that is added is automatically organized in such a way that Google will pick it up and display each new page and post automatically in its search results. These days, all WordPress sites also generate mobile optimized versions automatically.

Despite the prevalence of WordPress sites floating around online, you will still be able to create something that uniquely speaks to your target audience thanks to the wide variety of different templates that are available for use, both in free and paid versions. With a little thought and effort, you should be able to easily find one that will attract the type of customers that you are looking for. This doesn't mean that you can't create something from scratch if the mood strikes you, as you can create something totally unique as well. The personalization options don't end there, however, and WordPress also offers a wide variety of different plugins to add even more unique functionality to your site.

Start with the domain: Before you can go ahead and create a website, the first thing you are going to need to consider is what you are going to call it. It is important to put some thought into choosing the right name as you are going to want to pick something distinctive that also makes it clear what niche you are targeting and, if possible, an indication of what your unique point of view is going to be. If you can't manage something that is short and catchy in addition to all of the above, then you are going to want to consider a URL that references the site name or is indicative of it in some way.

With the name in mind, you will then want to register the domain name using any one of countless sites that offer these services. At this stage, it doesn't matter which you choose as they all perform the same function so picking the cheapest is the best option. Typically, you can find these services for around $1.

When it comes to choosing an extension, it may be tempting to branch out from .com if the URL you had your eye on was taken, but it is best to avoid doing so if at all possible. URL's that don't in with .com are typically seen as less legitimate than the alternative, plus any advertising you may ultimately end up doing could just end up driving traffic to a competitor's site as when most people think of a URL they assume it ends in .com anyway.

When choosing a name, it is also important to choose one that doesn't contain any needless punctuation and is also easy to grasp the spelling of when it is said aloud. In addition to making it harder for people to type in your URL directly, it also takes more work for sites with confusing URLs to reach the front page of a specific Google search result.

Hosting: Once you have registered a domain, the next thing you will need to do is to choose a website to host your site, along with all of the traffic that you will be bringing in. While there are plenty of different hosting options out there when you are first getting started you don't need to worry about anything too elaborate. In fact, something simple, such as the $5 a month plan from HostGator.com will more than meet your needs.

To set up hosting, all you need to do is to follow the onscreen instructions and then enter your domain name when prompted. You will then be given a password and username that you are going to want to keep on hand for the next step.

Getting started with WordPress: Many hosting companies provide the ability to install WordPress directly from their site with just a few clicks of the mouse. In order to get started, you will first need to log into the control panel (cPanel) using the username and password that you were provided in the last step. Once you have logged in you will want to find the page titled Software and Services before finding the option for WordPress and providing the requested information. Once you follow the onscreen prompts you will be provided with another username and password which will allow you to enter your WordPress site directly.

Tell the server where to look: After your new website is actually up and running, the only thing left to do is ensure that your domain name actually points where it needs to be. In order to ensure your domain point in the right direction, you are going to want to go back into the cPanel screen and find the option for nameserver details. You will know that you have found the right details if the information provided ends in the domain of the company that is hosting your site. You will want to write down this information before vising the domain site and entering it under the details for nameserver there.

Login: Once your nameserver is pointed to the right place, you are finally ready to access your site and personalize it in a way that suites your niche the best. To get to the backend of your site, all you need to do is type in the URL before appending it with/wp-admin. When prompted, enter your username and password and it is off to the races.

Choose the right theme: As you load up your page for the first time you will be greeted with the default WordPress theme which is called Twenty Eleven. Changing this theme is crucial to providing your site with its own identity and helping to build the confidence of your target audience as it shows that you are committed to the task at hand and that you aren't just some fly-by-night operation. There are thousands of themes available, many of them free so that you can get started without worrying about having to put any extra money down.

Choosing a theme that appeals to your target audience should be the first order of business and choosing one that is related to your niche is always a good idea as well. Modern website design leans heavily on the idea that less is more so something that is rather understated is a great way to start. Once you know what your theme is going to be you are going to want to pick out a few colors that compliment it as well as a no more than 3 different fonts to use throughout the site as a whole to keep it from feeling disjointed.

After you have chosen the theme that makes the most sense for your audience, you may be able to apply it directly, or you may need to download it and then upload it to your site directly. This can be done from the Appearance option that is found on the WordPress Dashboard, from there, simply look for the theme option. Once it is uploaded, all that is left is to install and you will be ready to go.

Once your theme is up and running, you will then want to look into the available options that may allow you to customize it even further. Common options include changes for the sidebar, footer and header. The footer is the header and footer are found at the top and bottom of each page respectively and the sidebar can show up on either the left or right of every page. These parts of the page typically contain things like the site logo, name of the site and menu options.

Particular customization options can be found on the Customize menu which is nested under the My Sites option. It is important to put some time into the choices you make here as they will often be the first things potential customers will see and interact with which means that they need to be positive across the board.

You will also want to take some time and modify the background of your site using either a personalized image or customized colors, both of which can be accessed from the same customize window. Remember, if you choose to upload your own image it is important to pick something that is relatively timeless and not overly loud as it can be easy to make a subpar first impression if you aren't careful.

Consider popular plugins: After you have chosen a theme that accurately reflects the niche and the target audience that you are looking to attract, one of the last things that you will need to do is install any plugins that you plan on using. Plugins add extra functionality to your site without forcing you to deal with the hassle of creating code from scratch. The following plugins are recommended to get you started though there are hundreds of more options that are both free and available for a small fee.

Aksimet: This plugin is useful for preventing span from reaching the comment section of any of the posts you create.

WordPress SEO: This plugin will go a long way towards improving the search engine optimization for the posts and pages that you create making it more likely that your page will be ranked highly on Google or Bing. This doesn't mean that you don't need to choose the right keywords, titles and descriptions, however.

Digg Digg: This useful plugin automatically adds the types of common social media buttons that you see on most sites making it more likely that visitors will share the information they like.

Contact Form 7: This plugin makes it easy for your target audience to get in touch with you directly.

Related content: This plugin is crucial because it will list other posts that users might enjoy at the end of each post, making them more likely to stick around than they otherwise might be.

Backup Buddy: This useful plugin automates the process of backing up your site to help prevent accidents.

Total Cache: This plugin is a must as it automatically improves the way your site performs by storing commonly used sections for faster loading.

WP Touch: This plugin is a must these days with so many individuals using mobile devices as it adds touch functionality to your site.

Pages or posts: WordPress automatically classifies all of its content as either pages or posts. Pages are primarily used for static, evergreen content, while posts are going to be more fluid. Generally speaking, if you are adding a new post, then you are adding it to a specific page. Pages tend to include things like your About Me page, a page that links to all the reviews you've done and also a page that compiles all of your posts in chronological order, starting with the newest. As an affiliate marketeer, you are going to want to set your homepage to your posts page.

Set up permalinks: It is important to take the time to set up permalinks as well as without them it will be hard for your target audience to return to posts a second time, say if they read your review and then thought about it some and are now ready to buy. By default, all of your links are going to have URLS that are a mix of letters and numbers, so turning on permalinks will also improve your SEO instead. You can set your URLs to include the name of the post by going to Settings and looking for the option for permalinks. There are several different options though either name or date are the most useful in most cases.

Utilize Google AdSense

By taking advantage of Google's advertising program you can exploit every single individual who visits your site via impression based targeted advertising. Additionally, if you include a search bar that works for the entirety of Google then any purchases that come from that search bar will be credited as your commission as well. This is a particularly useful feature if you are fond of comprehensive reviews as it can be a way to mitigate the fact that people tend to leave a comprehensive review without clicking through to a merchant site.

First up, you will need to choose the type of formatting for the ads that will naturally fit the layout of your website. According to Google, 160x600, 300x250 and 336x280 are the shapes that routinely see the best results. Additionally, it is important to keep in mind the color scheme of the ad you agree to so that it doesn't' clash with the rest of your site in a grating way. It is also important to keep in mind the best possible location for the ad as it is important to put it somewhere visible, while also ensuring it isn't the first thing that viewers to your site see as this will likely send them running for the hills. This means that the best place to start is going to be either the footer or the sidebar.

If you are interested in giving AdSense a try, you can download a plugin to set it up easily from the plugin installation menu where you traditionally add new add-ons. Search for the Google AdSense plugin and choose the option to install. Once the plugin has been installed you simply find the plugin list and choose the option to activate AdSense. You will then need to visit the plugin settings menu and chose the option to Get Started.

You can get started by first signing into the Google account that is connected to your website before then double checking that it can see your site. Assuming everything is good to go, you will then want to choose the option to verify. Once verification has been completed you can then activate it from the plugin settings. With this done, you will then be able to set up advertising options for both the primary and mobile version of your site. After AdSense is activated, you can then manage placement of individual ad by going to Settings and looking for the option to Manage Ads.

With this done, you will then want to choose the template that you will use for each ad as different ads can be attached to different templates. To look through potential templates, you will want to use the Review option which can be found near the Design button. This will allow you to preview the selected template, with the green boxes showing where the ads will ultimately be placed. You can add in three AdSense boxes at a time by placing an X next to the relevant locations. Make sure you save before exiting and you are reading to start profiting from clicks and views.

Chapter 6. Web Analytics

There are three fundamental ways to get essential data from Google: AdWords, Google Analytics, and Google Search Console. Each of these SEO pillars provides you with a wealth of knowledge that can be analyzed, interpreted, and used to inform an effective SEO strategy. We have already covered the AdWords Keyword Planner in detail.

Google Analytics (GA) is a tool that you can use to better understand your traffic and the behavior of your users while they are on your website. It can help you reverse engineer a perfectly optimized website from the ground up. Launching an SEO-friendly website is only half the game. You will also need to continually monitor your traffic and the health of your website, tweaking it for SEO indefinitely.

The key to succeeding in the new era of content-driven SEO is to understand how users search, where they come from, who they are, and how they interact with you on your website and with your content. When you consistently monitor your website performance, you will get a better idea about which strategies work and which do not work.

Understanding your website traffic is not just about SEO. You can also use this information to track and measure how your traditional marketing efforts are doing. For example, many advertising campaigns include a special-purpose landing page. But even marketing and advertising that does not point directly back to your website can result in visits.

Getting information on a traffic spike and your user data can help you refine and measure your ROI so that you can better manage your efforts. All roads in this book lead back to great content. It is your ability to use GA data to find and create great content which will set you apart from other companies.

The ability to look back at traffic, your user base, and where it is coming from allows you to create better, more targeted content for these individuals. With this data, content ideas are based on conversion instead of whim. You can also find sites that link to you, and use this referral tracking information to form new partnerships or create content distribution opportunities that you did not know existed.

The Exponential Power of Google Analytics

It is difficult to cover all of the features and benefits of GA here, because there are so many. There are entire books and educational training programs dedicated to teaching people how to use and interpret GA data. The only problem with GA is the abundance of information.

There are more ways to slice up and analyze the traffic on your website than there is information on your site. But there is exponential power in using GA to guide your SEO and other online marketing strategies for your website.

The traffic and user data GA provides can solve your website's content problems as they arise. You can also use it to regularly improve your content, through trial and error and test campaigns. And the insights you generate from GA data can lead to new goals, strategies, and tactics. You get a huge competitive edge when you focus on evidence-based SEO and content creation for your website.

Chapter 7. Dropshipping

Dropshipping is an element of retail fulfillment practice in the standard retail model that allows a store selling products and merchandise to not hold its own inventory; in other words, do away with keeping their products in stock, or shipping their products to their customers on their own or owning a warehouse to store its products. In this case, whenever there's an order for the product, the seller purchases its item from a third-party vendor and this third-party vendor ships it directly to the customer. This retailer partner with a dropship supplier does the manufacturing, warehousing, packaging, and shipping of these products on the retailer's behalf. The merchant doesn't see or handle the said product.

Who is Dropshipping For?

If you're a first timer entering the online business, then drop shipping is a great business model to begin with initially. It's low-risk and low-investment which is great for novices starting their business. It doesn't involve much monetary gamble. It's ideal for someone who is the current owner of a retail store and already has an inventory, but looking to reach newer, wider markets. This business model, however, doesn't give you amazing results from the get-go. Dropshipping margins are relatively lower so this might not bode well for a startup brand because these businesses do not have ultimate control where customer satisfaction related to brand experience and branding is concerned.

How much money can you potentially earn?

Depending on how much work you put into and the effort of time and some money, you can earn anywhere from $1,000 to $1,000,000 in a year or more. For example, if you get a product at $15 and you sell it on your site for $30. Minus the shipping and advertising costs, your profit is $10. To make $100,000 in a year, you need to sell at least 1000 products each month. This means $10 x 1000 orders = $10,000 per month. You can potentially earn $120,000 if your idea, product, and strategies work well.

How does Dropshipping work?

- Finding your Niche in Dropshipping - It may sound overwhelming to find your niche in business because there are plenty of things that you can get involved in at first. An evergreen niche is a niche that most retailers would like - it stands the test of time. Things like gaming, beauty, fashion, and weight loss are very evergreen niches. However, on the other hand, trending niches have instant profits and surge, but it also falls in popularity pretty fast.

- Looking and Finding the Right suppliers - In the world of dropshipping, it's critical to work with the right supplier, especially since suppliers are a crucial element of this entire drop shipping process. But like everything in life, drop shipping suppliers also come in different sizes, needs, and interests. To identify good suppliers is to place small orders to get a sense of their processes, sales reps, and professionalism. This way, you can pinpoint:

  - How efficient their ordering process is
  - How fast items are shipped out
  - How efficient they are in following up with an invoice for tracking information
  - How good the quality of their packing is

- Setting up your Business - One of the biggest pull factors is that you don't need stock or even to handle the things that you are selling and you can also start with limited funds. In its very basic idea, dropshipping requires a website optimized for e-commerce and ad from the merchant you purchase items from a third party supplier who then fulfills an order made by a customer on your e-commerce website. This cuts operational costs and also frees up your time to focus on other aspects of the business such as customer acquisition - marketing and promoting your website. A site optimized for e-commerce is extremely crucial in the drop shipping business model. One of the simplest platforms that you can use is Shopify, as it comes with built-in, customizable apps to help you create a website, increase sales, and even market your website. It's a very easy plug-and-play option.

Myths about Dropshipping

- Dropshipping only works for low priced, general products - The truth is, dropshipping now offers entrepreneurs looking to sell something the ability to offer specialized, high-quality items. If you find a niche for your products, you've definitely found a market that values quality products.

- You need to have an in-depth understanding of coding and all things IT-Any knowledge can be beneficial for your business but you don't need to be a tech-expert to run a dropshipping site. The basic idea of crafting a well working site as well as knowledge in marketing can help you kick off your business. Over time, as you gain knowledge and expertise as well as money, you can hire experts to help you fine-tune your business.

- All you need is to list products on your site and the sales will roll in - If that were true, then anyone can make a living with dropshipping. Unless you've hit the golden ticket with your product, chances of getting a profit immediately are quite dim. Dropshipping is not a get-rich scheme. It takes time to build and reach markets as well as target audiences. However, once you've got your footing, it'll be much easier.

Chapter 8. Passive Income and Advertising for Blogging Profit

The first place where you will want to work on affiliate marketing is on your own personal blog. Many people who have spent a few months, and sometimes a few years, building up a blog and gathering a large base of consistent readers, will choose to go with affiliate marketing to help them to monetize this blog. Since they already have the audience to do this, they can simply add the affiliate links into some of their content, and often they will get some clicks and some sales this way.

If you don't already have a blog, then now may be the best time to get one started. There are many different topics you can choose from, and you can easily be a way to create a blog, with lots of good content, based on the niche that you chose before. Of course, creating your own blog is not something that is going to happen overnight. It can take a lot of time and effort on your part, and you have to be ready to keep up with it, even once you have a good base of readers. Some of the steps that you can follow to do well with affiliate marketing include:

Pick out the niche you want to use for your blog. You can choose from many different options. Remember that you will be writing on this topic for a long time to come, so make sure that you are able to enjoy the topic and one you won't be sick writing on within a few months.

Pick out a domain name and hosting. You want to go with a name that relates to your niche and is also easy for your readers to remember. This can help with some of the SEO that you will want to work with later on. The hosting is also important because it can help you to pick out the right platform, the right add-ins, and more.

Start writing. The best way to get a blog to gain more followers is to start writing. You should start a consistent writing schedule now and get the hang of it, so it sticks once more readers join the group. You can't just post on occasion or sporadically, or it becomes very hard to keep your readers coming back for more.

Set up the SEO. This helps your potential readers to find you online and through search engines. If you don't get this set up the right way and pick the right keywords, it could be very hard for the readers to find you, and you won't be able to grow your following.

Of course, this is a process that can take some time and effort to do effectively. You won't be able to write for just a week or two and expect to have 100,000 followers. But if you can work hard and consistently on your blog, the followers will come, and you will be able to turn this into a great source of income.

Now that the blog is set up, after a few months or more, you can start to work with affiliate marketing on the page. Some of the steps that you can take in order to work with affiliate marketing with your website include:

Choose the Right Affiliate Marketing Program

The most important thing that you can do when you want to add affiliate marketing to your website is to choose the right program. Affiliate ads are going to be pay per action, the more relevant your links or ads are to your content, the more clicks you will get, and the more money you can make in the process.

So that leads us to the question, what type of affiliate program is going to work the best for your page and lead to the most clicks? If you have a focused topic on your blog, then you want to find affiliates that can associate and meet up with that content. An example of this is if you have a photography business, you may choose to use affiliate links to camera equipment or someone who sells this equipment.

Many bloggers find that it works well to start on Amazon Associates. This is because Amazon already sells millions of unique products, and this provides the blogger with a lot of choices in picking out the thing that works the best for them. And since Amazon offers a commission that is somewhere between four to fifteen percent, depending on the product type and the volume, you can make a good amount of money on it in the process.

Of course, there are going to be a lot of other options that you can choose from when it comes to picking out a good affiliate link. The trick here is to find a balance between having a good company with good commissions and lots of products to choose from, and one that meets your niche but doesn't have too much competition associated with it.

An Affiliate Aggregator May Be a Good Idea

If you find that the topics on your blog are kind of diverse, then working with an affiliate aggregator, such as VigLink, a system that can automate access to 30,000 affiliate programs for you while monetizing the links that you place on your site, maybe the right option for you.

In addition, to help monetize some of the links that you already have on your block, this automation tool can also optionally insert new and ordinary links in your content if there weren't any links there before. So, if you have some content that calls out a certain product or store, the automation service would add in the link for you and make sure that you got paid for any clicks and purchases that may occur.

You will find that this is a great way to make sure you are getting the most out of your blog. Since it can take a lot of time and effort to go through and add in all of these links on your own, using an affiliate aggregator will ensure that you get the most out of all this, without having to put in all the legwork or worrying that you missed out on something along the way.

Create Some Content that Will Actually Sell

You don't want to work with content that is boring and will turn your customer away. Many bloggers will find unique ways to write information and content that helps to sell the products to their readers. For example, you may choose to write out a review of a product, or you can provide different solutions to your customers, or even do a comparison for a few different products. The more creative you can be here, the easier it is for you to make some money on that link.

The power that comes with a blog is that it is easy to collect a ton of fans for a niche and a specific topic. This lends itself really well to making recommendations and providing the links that go with those recommendations. But just adding in these links to a product, without any rhyme or reason behind it, can mean that you may get a lot of clicks, but quick exits with no sales.

Your job here is to write out some content that will actually help to sell the product. Don't just put up a list of books, for example, and then hope that people will click on them and make a purchase. Instead, write out a review of the books or write about them in some way, and then point the reader in the right direction if they are interested in purchasing it.

Integrate Affiliate Links in the Right Way

If you do decide to add these links to your site, make sure that there is some balance between the user experience that you provide and the monetization that you try to get. One way to do this is to still keep your content ad-free as much as possible.

There is nothing wrong with having a link in place on a few articles. But if you are doing this on each page that you have, and you add in a ton of links into each one, the reader is going to realize this and find the content less engaging. Your readers won't mind hearing about a product on occasion, but if you are doing it all the time, they will see that you just want money, rather than helping them, and they will leave.

Affiliate marketing can lend itself well to blogs. You already have a big market for people who are interested in what you have to say and the recommendations that you provide to them. When you take advantage of this, in a way that will still provide a good experience to the user, you will be able to see some amazing results with earning money off your blog.

Chapter 9. The Most Important Tips for Success in Affiliate Marketing

Yes, there are a lot to reap, but do not forget that you have to work for them. Do not ever entertain the misconception that you will be wealthy overnight from this racket.

Although this job can definitely be lucrative and also a great way makes money via the Internet, it is also just as competitive. There are a lot of other affiliate marketers out there who are competing for the exact same market that you are targeting.

Consistency is key to success with affiliate marketing.

You must be consistent when working affiliate marketing. If you are only going to put in 7 hours a week toward your affiliate marketing business, make it be 1 hour per day, not 7 hours in one day because it comes through consistent application of marketing strategies. Set up a time each day to work on it and stick to your plan.

So, for you to be a successful affiliate marketer, you have to understand a couple of things. This includes the needs of your target market, proper product promotion and other strategies that have been proven to work in the practice. To help you with that, here are some tricks that other successful affiliate marketers have applied, and you might as well try for yourself, too.

Choose only a handful of good products

To begin with, you should be careful in your choice of products that you will promote or market. In this regard, one of the biggest mistakes commonly committed by new affiliate marketers—and even some of the old ones as well—is that they register with a whole lot of affiliate programs. Then they try to promote all the available products.

This is a big no-no. It will greatly affect your concentration, which in turn, will have an impact on your performance. It is like juggling a number of jobs. You cannot get a hold of them all. It will be too overwhelming. You will have your hands full and the chances are, you will not be able to promote even a single product properly.

While multitasking is possible, some people do not realize the dangers of overdoing it. Yes, you can register in more than one affiliate program and market a couple of items. But do not grab everything in sight.

You have to keep in mind that in order to be successful in this field, all you have to do is work with only a handful of good products—with emphasis on the good right there. You will be amazed that even a little of these great products can already make you earn way more than what you can get if you promote a multitude of products.

This is because good products are not hard to sell. The consumers and shoppers themselves are the ones looking for ways to buy them. But of course, you still have to do your part and launch an equally good Internet marketing work. Keep in mind that there are a lot of other affiliate marketers competing for the same market.

So, when you choose the products you will promote, the best practice is to know and understand the needs of your target market. At the same time, you should also search for goods that will perfectly align with the topic of your affiliate site.

This is a smart way of making money. You do not tire yourself too much, but still do the proper actions to get all the necessary work done and earn money.

Use a couple of traffic sources for product promotion

One of the common mistakes that some affiliate marketers commit is that they put advertisements and other promotional materials only in their sites. Although there is nothing wrong with this practice, you must also know that there are a lot of other sources that you can tap into in order to generate traffic and market products at the same time. It will be much better if you take a look at this for, they will not only make your job easier, but also increase your chances of getting your clients to make a purchase. Keep in mind that the more traffic you generate to the host company's site and sales page, your chances of making a larger sum of money will also increase.

A good example that you can use is Google Adwords. Here, all you have to do is make an advertisement in your Adwords account. Afterwards, use the affiliate link provided to you and put it in the target page URL of the ad you made. Then you will have to measure the conversions continuously. It is important to see if the campaign you mounted costs less than the profit you are expecting to earn. If that is the case, then said campaign is definitely worth running.

Test, measure and track your campaign

While using different strategies for product promotion is highly recommended, you must also not forget to monitor the progress of your project. This way, you will clearly see which techniques are giving you good results and which ones simply do not work. And with that, you can make an assessment to know what appropriate actions you should take.

In this regard, you can try split testing. This will help you adequately measure the performance of the campaigns you have mounted.

Once you get the results of the assessment, you can begin making some tweaks here and there. As studies and actual practice have shown, this can significantly increase your profits.

At the same time, it is also a good idea to put the banner advertisements in different areas in your site. Put them in various pages. And in each page, vary their locations as well. The underlying principle here is that some positions or areas will make the advertisements more conspicuous or noticeable than the others.

If your host company or affiliate program provides you basic statistics, make use of them. They will be helpful empirical data for your strategy planning. However, do not make the provided statistics serve as a limitation to you. Here are other conversions tracking software readily available for you. You can even make your own to track your affiliate campaign.

Keep yourself and your campaigns updated

The Internet has an ever-changing landscape. Hence, trends continuously change. With that, it is important that you as an affiliate marketer keep up with the latest techniques and strategies. Keep up with the times. Make sure that you know and understand the latest styles and tools in the marketing field. Otherwise, you will be left out while other affiliate marketers go on to progress.

So, once you know the latest trends, plan your strategy around it. Observe and make an assessment. Keep in mind that you do not have to apply every new trend. Again, the ability to discern those that will work for you is important. Do not grab everything in sight.

Update your methods and techniques every now and then so that the consumers will not get bored. Keep in mind that they are constantly looking for something new. Hence, that is what you should give to them to catch their attention and investment.

Work with the right merchant

Affiliate marketing has a lot to do with making the right choices. This is true not just in terms of products, but also when it comes to merchants. Bear in mind that you will be marketing not just the products, but also the brand. Hence, you have to make it a point to pick a reputable company merchant. Again, smart choices.

You will also be putting your reputation on the line. When you put an ad in your affiliate site, it is already an outright personal recommendation to your visitors to patronize said brand or product. And of course, you do not want to disappoint your visitors by making them buy a particular product which made them unhappy eventually. With that, your credibility gets tarnished.

Every time this happens, less people will take your advice or recommendation. It lowers customer satisfaction. And that will hurt your reputation in the long run. If you plan to establish a career in affiliate marketing, that would signal your downfall.

So, to avoid this, think wisely early on and work with credible companies and businesses. This way, you will be promoting good products that will be able to meet the demands of your clients. Hence, they will continue to patronize your site, and this will be a good investment on your part.

Pick useful tools

Lastly, make things much easier for yourself by finding and using tools that will make your work more efficient. Remember, it is all about working smart. You do not have to tire yourself by working too hard if there are ways to achieve the same results with less work. One of which is through using Internet marketing tools. There are actually a lot of them out there.

Say for instance your affiliate site is powered by WordPress. You may as well consider getting a plug-in that is similar to the Affiliate Link Manager.

The bottom line here is that it will be much better for you to devote your time searching for useful aids and tools then mastering them, so you work more efficiently to achieve good results. This is the initial step. Then in the long run, you will see the benefits starting to manifest in terms of work convenience coupled with higher commission.

Strategies To Generate Traffic

You will be focused on generating traffic. Although this is the last that does not mean that it is the least significant aspect of the job. Contrary to that, generating traffic is one of the first but most important steps in affiliate marketing.

But first, what does generate traffic mean? Essentially, it is about getting Internet users and consumers to visit the website or page of your host merchant. The traffic referred to here is the consumer traffic or the people visiting the website.

And in affiliate marketing, you should always take note of the fact that it is your job to get a whole lot of targeted traffic in order to be successful. At the same time, you should also keep in mind that not all the visitors of your affiliate site will click on the links and banner advertisements.

With that, it becomes much more important for you to get more traffic by mixing and spicing up your marketing strategy. In this regard, you do not have to fret because there are actually a multitude of tactics that you can use. As a beginner, here are some that you can use.

Search Engine Optimization

Good rankings in search engine results pages lead to organic and highly targeted traffic that has higher chances of conversion. You could outsource SEO tasks or do it yourself.

Paid advertising

For one, there is paid advertising. This strategy is deemed to be the most effective when the headline of your advertisement copy, graphics or message calling consumers to action just come together strongly in order to persuade consumers to click the links and make a purchase.

Free advertising

Then there is free advertising. This is just like the first one, except that there are no fees. But of course, you cannot expect the same high quality and leeway. For this strategy, you can make use of sites like US Free Ads and Craigslist. These are two of the most famous sites that accept banner advertisements and links free of charge.

Article marketing

This is one of the most popular and widely used Internet marketing methods today. One reason for this is the fact that it offers quite a lot of benefits. For one, you will be building your reputation as a credible source in the niche you are working on. You will also gain a higher ranking in search engines as the number of links that lead to your site also increases. Given all that, more traffic will be generated to your affiliate site.

Chapter 10. Step by Step On How to Practice Affiliate Marketing

Reach Out to Customers Using Various Methods

With the ability to generate a lot of cash and drive sales, affiliate marketing is a cost-effective and powerful lead generation tactic where brands and businesses pay solely for performance. According to Google Trends, over the past few years, online searches for affiliate marketing have increased, likely from both affiliates and brands that are planning to leverage the tactic to maximize their earnings. Some interesting statistics about this performance-based marketing approach include:

1. In the US, affiliate marketing spend is expected to surpass $6 billion by 2020.

2. Experts expect it to grow at an annual compound rate of 10%.

3. More than 80% of brands use this marketing approach to generate more sales, engage with existing customers, and capture consumers' attention.

4. 79% of marketers use it to drive conversions.

Affiliate marketing can help individuals take advantage of the power of influence by collaborating with several affiliates to tap into potentially profitable audiences. However, growing one's audience is not as easy as it may sound. It takes a great marketing strategy, time, and effort to bring the best results. Due to the high level of competition in this market nowadays, an affiliate marketer may need to use multiple sources to reach out to customers.

Many large companies work with affiliate marketers to maximize their sales, but not all of them employ the same sources to boost demand and visibility for their products. Affiliates can leverage many different marketing channels and strategies. Some of the most effective affiliate marketing approaches that can help grow an individual's audience include:

Partner with the right affiliates

Affiliate marketers can take advantage of the power of influence to expand their audiences and get potential customers to click on their affiliate links and make a purchase. They can influence their audiences purchasing decisions by working with marketers who have a large and engaged audience that believes in them. When choosing an affiliate to partner with, it is important to determine whether or not:

a) They have a high site ranking, loyal following, engagement, views, and authority

b) They are in the same niche market

c) They have a good relationship with their audiences

This is necessary to ensure that one's efforts are successful. For example, if an individual were to promote a particular food product, collaborating with a coupon site that gives discounts on electronic products would not make any sense. Instead, one should choose affiliates in the food market to gain more leads with minimum effort.

Use promotions from many sources

One should take the time to reach out to one's audience through affiliate promotions and marketing strategies from other sources. This will help one discover which audience is easier to reach and responds the best. Some great sources to take advantage of include:

a)   Email marketing: Email marketing involves sending out emails to people on your contact list and beyond. It will require you to come up with an appealing email, a compelling message, and a call to action. You want the readers of the email to follow the link you will provide to get to your website and possibly make a purchase. The biggest challenge in this form of marketing is that some of the recipients might label your emails as spam, and therefore make it hard for people to read any of your future emails. If you have a long list of email subscribers, it would be wise to use this form of marketing to interact with them in order to drive more conversions.

b)   Product reviews: Are you one of those people who always scroll down to read what people have to say about a particular product before buying it? If you do so, know that most, if not everyone who makes online purchases do the same. If your website has a customer feedback section and product review section, then you are on the right track. On the other hand, using a product review blog to promote your products and/or services can lead to even greater efficiency. Such blogs tend to attract people who are really interested in buying something.

c) Using YouTube videos: YouTube is the biggest online video platform in the world and one of the websites with the highest number of users in the world. This means that millions of potential clients are on YouTube and using videos to promote your products will surely help you to drive up your sales, in addition to expanding your audience. In fact, about 40% of millennials say that some YouTube personalities seem to understand them better than most of their friends.

Using multiple sources to reach out to one's customers can help one achieve the best results from one's marketing strategies. This will also help one discover the platform or source where one's audience and potential customers are most engaged. Conversions will not happen overnight. One needs to choose the right channels, affiliates, and marketing strategies to boost conversions.

How to Make Use of Coupons, Deals, And Promotions

As a business owner, company or individual, offering affiliates a small incentive to market your products is a great way to drive sales. Using affiliates increases your online presence because of the traffic redirected to your site.

An affiliate can be an individual or a company. The work of affiliates is to market your products by posting them on their websites, blogs, social media pages or any other place they have online influence. Business owners can maximize the potential of their affiliate marketers by working with them to offer customers coupons, deals, and promotions.

97% of consumers like getting discounts when they go out shopping, so they are likely to shop through sites that offer coupons, deals, and promotions. A smart business owner will not only use affiliate sites but also look for the ones that make use of coupons, deals, and promotions to attract even more customers.

A number of affiliate sites have dedicated tools for managing coupons, deals, and promotions. Affiliate sites not only advertise to the incoming traffic on their websites, but they also maintain contact information of their customers to whom they can send anything from periodic newsletters to promotion deals.

Coupons

A coupon is a small piece of paper that allows its owner to get discounts off a certain product and pay less money for the product. A large number of consumers like using coupons while shopping.

However, having to cut them out of magazines and newspapers and remembering to carry them every time has discouraged a few people from enjoying the benefits of coupons. Luckily, the Internet has simplified the process and online coupons are now fast and easy to use. Those who did not enjoy the chore of cutting out coupons can now find and use coupons with just a few clicks.

If giving out coupons makes sense for your business, then all you have to do is look for an affiliate site that uses this marketing strategy. Dealing directly with coupon websites may be impossible. Most of them are accessible through affiliate networks who act as intermediaries to handle negotiations, track sales and manage payments.

Once the merchant and the affiliate reach an agreement, the coupon website will receive and display your coupons in categories as well as advertise special discounts on their homepage. A coupon site should be well versed with search engine optimization to attract new customers. They maintain a mailing list.

In most cases, a merchant will only pay the affiliate coupon site their commission if and only if an actual conversion or sale has been made.

Deals

Aside from dropping prices through the use of coupons, traders can present consumers with deals. By giving deals on their products and services, merchants can attract more customers.

Deals are normally valid for a specified period usually shorter than the validity period of a coupon. They can range from cash discounts, percentage discounts, free shipping to free gifts. Research shows that 92% of consumers shop looking for deals.

An affiliate site normally allows merchants to dictate the parameters of the deal. With such tools, a merchant can advertise for a certain deal as well as specify details like the start and expiration date of a deal.

Depending on the affiliate network a merchant decides to go with, the merchant can enjoy several features offered by this tool. Some affiliate networks allow other affiliates not linked to a merchant to see a deal and therefore get into business with the merchant and bring him more sales while others may offer a Deal of the Day tool specific for advertising deals.

Deals can appear on the affiliate's homepage or the affiliate can write an email to subscribers informing them of a particular offer.

Promotions

A promotion is a short-term marketing strategy that creates urgency to drive sales up. Coupons and deals can be incorporated into sales promotion. Other examples of sales promotions include flash sales, buy one get X free, and free samples.

People advertise promotions the same way they advertise coupons and deals. Depending on the affiliate site, there are tools to dictate the promotion parameters and a customer can only claim a commission after the sale goes through the affiliate's site.

Some affiliate websites offer tracking tools and software to monitor the progress of a promotion.

Voucherify is an example of a software that creates and tracks promotions.

Settling on the right affiliate site

As much as people love using coupons, getting great deals and saving on promotions merchants should be cautious especially where affiliate marketers are involved. They should:

- Carry out extensive research to find out what deals the competitors are offering. The merchant can either match them or offer better ones.
- Make use of search engines to look for the appropriate affiliate websites that are dominant in a specific industry. Affiliate websites that appear on the first and second pages of a Google search are a safer choice.
- Go an extra mile and try the customer experience. The merchant should try using a coupon or participating in a promotion and take note of the experience.
- Check out the traffic of customers visiting the affiliate site.

Leveraging on rewards is one of the most effective strategies for boosting conversions. Every consumer loves a good deal that will help him or her save money on his or her purchases. Therefore, you can capitalize on the need for a client to look for discount vouchers and deals before purchasing a product and/or service and this will surely lead to profits. Tons of deals and coupon websites that allow affiliates to attract more potential customers by offering a good discount exist. This is most common in markets such as electronic gadgets, travel, beauty, and food.

Product Page Optimization

Due to the fast-paced growth of the eCommerce world, optimization has become one of the most popular buzzwords in the industry. The rapid advancement of technology and fluidity of consumer demand have forced online businesses to stay alert, optimizing or improving their websites to enhance customer engagement and for SEO purposes.

Though the eCommerce market is experiencing tremendous growth, many businesses are still struggling to boost their conversion rates. Most focus on optimizing their carts and checkout pages and forget about one of the most important pages, i.e., the product page. In fact, most customers will not even get to the cart and checkout pages if the product page fails to grab their attention. They will leave the store after checking out the product pages. Therefore, it is extremely important to create attention-grabbing, high-converting product pages.

The product page is mostly a combination of tons of programming and a little customization. Many product pages are similar to the options available with common shopping cart systems, which is unfortunate. A good product page needs to make an immediate and positive impression since it is often where important choices are made on whether to make a purchase or not. Product page optimization, therefore, is meant to help boost conversion rates.

An optimized product page

Simply put, this is a product page, which is designed and customized to not only convert visitors into customers but also to rank well on search engines. SEO will significantly boost one's Internet business, especially in the current competitive online market. All types of online businesses, including affiliate marketing, can benefit from product page optimization and SEO. Appearing in the first page of a prominent search engine is the end-goal of optimization, and although it is achievable, there is nothing easy about it. Common ways of optimizing product pages for better results include the below.

Displaying one's products from multiple angles

It is important to show one's products from different angles using high-quality imagery to capture potential customers' attention. People love having the exact picture of what they are buying and presenting it in the best possible way is a great idea. You can also enhance the impact further by adding some context. For example, in addition to showing a particular product, such as a dress, from different angles, the product page can also display it with the accessories that make up the photo, e.g., a necklace. Although the central product highlighted in this case is the dress, featuring the necklace on either side of the dress might increase conversions. However, it should not distract from the central item.

Understand trust signals

These tiny symbols at the bottom of product pages announce to visitors that an individual's site is virus-free and secure, or that the site has a rating of five stars on a vendor directory. These signs help visitors to your site to feel secure to browse around and possibly even make a purchase. Other trust signals are those that deal with any possible consumer concerns even before they choose to make a purchase. They include answers to matters such as:

- Shipping
- Expected time of arrival
- Shipping costs
- Wish lists
- Other customers' experiences with the product
- Nice, little touches

When it comes to Internet commerce, little touches on one's product pages can make a huge difference. In fact, they may very well play a key role in convincing customers to commit. Most of the times online shoppers look for the smallest excuses or even details to leave a website and look for another one that they will feel confident enough to buy from. Something like excellent customer support can be all it takes to win over a nervous shopper. However, customers do not want to sign-up for something in order to get support.

Get rid of checkout anxieties

Nipping certain customer anxieties in the bud can ultimately help close the sale. As often as possible, ask friends to go over your page and give you feedback concerning things that might make them want to check out, as well as those that make them feel comfortable to stay. For example, customers will be more likely to buy if they are confident in the product's compatibility. They might also want a synopsis of the product or a confirmation that the security seals will work.

Make product pages printer friendly

This should be obvious to someone who wants to venture in affiliate marketing; however, many product pages still do not offer a print-friendly option. This is especially helpful to customers who are on the go and want to show a particular product to their family members or friends. It is also helpful to those who want to look at a large image rather than use the small screens on their mobile devices.

Provide adequate product content

In addition to providing good product images, a great product page should provide detailed information about each product, since that is the main reason the page actually exists. This information will inform site visitors about a product's features and benefits, which can help drive them to make a purchase. This information should provide details such as:

- Product price – Be very specific and offer a currency converter for the sake of clients outside your country.
- Capacity, size, and dimensions – Be very specific and consider visitors who use the metric system of measurement, in case you use the imperial system.
- Relevant product title – This will help the visitors identify the product quickly and with the least hassle.
- Brand information – Provide as much brand information as possible, even though the manufacturer will do a lot here.
- Components and features – Make sure to highlight any components and features your visitors and potential buyers will consider relevant.

- Maintenance and care instructions – This is very important because the visitors will want to know what they can do in case they encounter some challenges during use

Product material

Optimize for Mobile

Without a doubt, mobile Internet commerce is growing faster and larger everyday thanks to the exponential growth of the use of mobile devices. These days, people want to browse the Internet using their mobile phones, as opposed to waiting until they get to their computers to do so. Recently, Google launched its mobile-first indexing update, and this means that product pages that do not meet the standard optimization standards for mobile devices will likely lose sales, traffic, and revenue. Mobile-friendly product pages can help businesses:

Improve customer experiences

Provide faster checkouts through mobile or digital wallets

Give customers the ability to buy anytime and from anywhere

Boosting the product page's load speed is also important. Businesses with slow conversion rates due to their poor product pages should, therefore, take a serious look at their eCommerce system and its functionality. By adding the features outlined above, they will significantly increase their conversion rates, in addition to creating well-rounded shopping experiences that every customer will value.

Make Use of Influencers and Bloggers

Influencer and blogger marketing are a growing trend used in online business, public relations campaigns, and other initiatives. This is the process of identifying, engaging, and working with people who create conversations with a business or brand's customers. Recently, this marketing strategy has mostly used social media as a channel of communication, giving an opportunity for businesses to promote their products and/or services through influencers or bloggers. According to Forbes, this type of marketing focuses mainly on specific individuals rather than the target market. Businesses hope that by working with people of interest, customers will be more willing to listen and try the products and/or services the companies offer.

As technology and media become more advanced, many people are now opting to promote products and/or services through branded content on Twitter, Facebook, Snapchat, and other personal social media accounts. More than ever before, people are looking to others to help inform their buying decisions. This has opened up a new opportunity for businesses to connect with their customers more organically and directly. If one is not leveraging this marketing strategy, now may be the time to do it. Influencers and bloggers are on the rise, making them one of the most powerful public relations and marketing trends of modern times.

Chapter 11. Step by Step On How to Practice Social Media Advertising

Social Media Marketing, or for short, SMM is a form of internet-based marketing that incorporates a variety of social media networks to achieve branding and marketing targets and goals. SMM involves the activities of sharing content, videos, and images socially, for marketing purposes. Brian Solis, a digital analyst, author, and speaker created a social media chart known as The Conversation Prism to categorize social platforms into various services and types of social media.

Social media is an essential component of a person's online life. With each new year, there are new social websites and applications that make social communication even more profound. Businesses use social media to promote brands, market products, connect with customers, expand reach, and influence and build new business ties.

The following exemplifies a variety of terms commonly associated with social media marketing and are essential, so you'll be able to use them effectively in your online marketing campaign:

Social Media Analytics- one of the primary reasons why social media marketing is an arsenal for any marketer is the fact that data can be obtained easily and quickly. Social Media analytics is all about gathering data from social media websites and blogs. This data is analyzed to enable marketers to make better decisions for their businesses and brands. Social media analytics is commonly used to assess customer sentiment towards a product or service and how their reactions can support marketing and customer service activities. Social Media Marketing reaps the benefits of social networking to enable a company to increase its brand recognition and presence as well as expand its customer reach. Social Media Marketing's goal is also to continuously stay relevant by creating compelling content that will prompt users to share what they have to say on their own social networks.

Social Media Marketing also includes social media optimization (SMO), and it works similarly to SEO, search engine optimization, except with SMO, the main goal is to attract unique visitors to a website via social networks.

There are two main ways of handling SMO which embody:

Adding social media links to content such as 'Tweet it' buttons, RSS feeds, sharing buttons, and Pin It buttons

Promoting activities through social media via tweets, pins, blog posts, and status updates

Social CRM, also known as Social Customer Relationship Marketing, is another powerful business tool that marketers use. When a visitor to your social network 'likes' or 'follows' you, this action opens a host of communication, marketing, and networking opportunities. Social media sites enable a customer to follow conversations about your company and brand in real-time, and the company receives market data and feedback.

Social Media CRM works both ways. It further enables a customer to tell a company and everyone about their experiences with the company's products or services, both good and bad experiences. For the business perspective, it allows them to respond in real-time to both these positive and negative feedback, attend to customer problems almost immediately, as well as rebuild or regain customer confidence. How a brand reacts is imperative to the overall future and growth of a company.

Enterprise Social Networking, on the other hand, encourages a company to connect people who have similar business interests or activities. For a company's employees, it enables them to access resources and information that they would require to work together effectively and solve business issues and problems.

Public social media platforms also enable businesses to stay connected with their customers, and it makes it easier for them to conduct research where this data can be used to enhance their business process and operations.

Crowdsourcing. Of late, social media is also popularly used for crowdsourcing. Crowdsourcing is the practice of gathering information, data, ideas, and even funds as a community towards a common goal.

How to Create a Social Media Marketing Plan

Without a shadow of a doubt, we all know how crucial social media marketing is in today's world. Things keep changing and evolving- without using new media tools that come into our lives to innovate, upgrade, update, and stay relevant.

Before you embark on social media marketing, a little bit of investment in research and a plan is always a good idea. Here are the most relevant steps when creating that perfect social media marketing campaign:

Start with A Reason

Your plans should start with listing out your reasons for having social media accounts. What is it that you want to achieve? What are your targets? Who is your audience? Where do they hang out? Do they even use social media? What do you want to say to them? With your team, brainstorm your reasons- if you do not already have some. Your current business plans using conventional or traditional marketing tools would already give you a good sense of what you are trying to achieve. From there on, write down your reasons and connect them with your targets and goals.

Develop your objectives & goals

SMM can help with a variety of marketing goals such as:

- Growing your website traffic
- Building conversions across different interest groups
- Increasing brand awareness
- Creating strong brand characteristics & personality and positive brand relationship
- Improving communication and relations with major audiences and influencers
- Only when you establish your goals will you be able to achieve and measure your ROI for social media.

To ensure you stay aligned with your goals when establishing your social media marketing across different types of networks, here are some essential tips for you to remember:

Planning – Do a keyword search and brainstorm for ideas that will attract and engage your targeted audience.

Content— Consistent content reigns supreme when it comes to SMM. Ensure that you offer valuable information that your audience will find interesting to the point where they want to share, like, link, or comment on your posts. Use images, videos, quotes, infographics, and even GIFs to compliment your text-based content.

Consistent- While each platform has its own unique audience, environment, and voice. Use these differences to tailor your messages, but always keeping in mind that your messages need to be consistent across all platforms.

Blog- Having a blog and a website enables you to share a wide variety of content. Blogs are relatively easier to maintain and make sharing information such faster. Your company blog is part of your social media marketing campaign because any recent social media efforts, activities, events, and promos will be highlighted in your blog.

Links- It isn't social media marketing if there's no sharing of your unique, original content to reach out to your current followers and gaining new ones. Linking content from other parties and organizations is also part of SMM.

Tracking Competitors- Tracing your competitor's activities can give you valuable insight into keyword research and other social marketing media stats. If your competitors are using social media and you aren't doing any of it, then it's something that you get going on as well- just do it better!

Analytics- What would social media marketing or traditional marketing for that matter be, if it weren't giving you some form of data? The successes of your campaigns are determined by the data you get. Google Analytics, Facebook, Instagram, and Twitter Insights all have analytics that helps you measure and track your social media input so you would be able to monitor them.

Conduct an Audit on Your Social Media

You need to assess your current situation with your social media use and how it's been working out for you so far. it's always beneficial to go back to the drawing block and to revise, change, and mix things up with your social media because after all, things change quickly. What campaigns worked for you before may not work so well now.

Conducting a social media audit includes determining who is currently connecting with you on social media, which sites your primary target market uses mainly and how your presence as a brand on social media differs from that of your competitors. HootSuite has created a social media audit template that you can use to process this information.

Chapter 12. The Top Tools

Tools help you make the best of your time and effort when it comes to marketing. We will look at the tools to help you make full use of your time, efficiently market your site and promote, your affiliations online. Most tools listed here give you a free version (with limited capabilities) or a trial version before requiring you to purchase the full license to use.

If you feel like this tool has met your needs, then sign up for a full package.

- Flippa

This essential tool can help you get into the process of building a sustainable and successful affiliate site from scratch. This site is created as a bidding marketplace for people to buy and sell websites. For affiliate marketers especially, you get to buy sites that already come with strong backlinks and an optimized SEO growth. Keep in mind that you need to conduct a full backlink audit before you purchase a domain from Flippa to ensure that the domain isn't inflated by unethical SEO practices.

- CJ Affiliate

Affiliate marketing begins with a strong partnerships with sites that are in need of sales. CJ Affiliates is a number one resource for affiliate partnerships as it connects affiliates with merchants wanting to drive up sales for their products. Affiliates get paid for each phone call, or lead, or website when visitors peruse a merchant's site from the affiliate links discovered. CJ Affiliate is a great starting point if you want to seek partnerships.

- SEMRush

If you are looking for keyword research, competition analysis and even fixing SEO errors then SEMRush is a tool needed in your affiliate marketing arsenal. This tool is a favorite among marketers who want to understand what kind or type of content drives the highest ROI for their competitors as well as analyze on-page SEO issues. What's more, you can use SEMRush to monitor press mentions.

- Ahrefs

Ahrefs is another keyword research tool that you can use just like SEMRush. It also provides on-page audits and competitive content analysis. What's different with Ahrefs is that it places a deeper emphasis on backlinks than on-page SEO. Ahrefs gives marketers insights about lost as well as new backlinks as well as sites that are linked to broken pages on your site. Marketers will find it useful to use Ahrefs for reviewing new and lost backlinks, assessing competitor link profiles, and also obtaining new link building opportunities.

You can also use Ahrefs to find sites that are linked to broken pages and of course finding top-performing competitor content. You can try out both SEMRush as well as Ahref's to build on your SEO optimization. If you can invest in both- great but if you cannot then think about what you really want to track first. If you are an industry leader in your niche, SEMRush would prove to be worthwhile. Since both SEMRush and Ahref have trial periods for their software, you can use both and see which works best for you.

- Yoast SEO

Yoast SEO gives you advanced SEO functionality in each and every page which includes the title tag and meta description which you can customize, canonical link customization, sitemap customization as well as meta robots customization. Yoast is a free tool; but if you want 24/7 support, then you can go for the paid version. They also have a redirect manager in the paid version that allows you to redirect broken pages or pages that you want to be removed from search results.

- Grammarly

This example exemplifies another useful tool to have if you are publishing content on a regular basis. It is good to have a tool that can check your spelling, grammar as well as plagiarism all in one go. Grammarly is a master-class tool in spell-check and grammar. It sports incorrect word use as well as comma usage. All in all, it makes your written content even better.

- Duplichecker

If you are part of the content team for your website, then running your article through Duplichecker will help you spot any kind of plagiarism. Of course Grammarly also does this task, but if your intention is only to check plagiarism, then Duplichecker is a good investment tool. Accidental cases of plagiarism can prove to be a painful legal issue, so it's best to get your content checked.

- Hemingway

Another amazing content review tool, Hemingway, helps you to simplify your writing. It is based off the writing style of Ernest Hemingway, hence the name of the software. Whatever content you write, especially the ones that go on the Internet, needs to be simple, straightforward and easy to understand. Your readers what the point to come across fast and their want insights, which means you do not want fluff tossed into your content just to make your sound intelligent. With the Hemingway software, you can simplify complex sentence, and it also points out complex words and adverbs that you can replace with simple ones.

- Sumo

One of the main things you want your site to do is attract visitors and with Suno, you turn your visitors into customers. Most website visitors are not ready to open their wallets and make a purchase with their credit cards when they reach your site, especially if it is their first time visiting. How can you possible get money from them? You sell them things that they are ready to buy. The best way most successful affiliate marketers do is to scale to build their email list. This enables marketers to drive repeat visitors back to their site and also to purchase products over a period of time. With Sumo, you can have easy to install email capture forms on your site.

- Google Adsense

Earning money for each referral you get is wonderful isn't it? Want to elevate this experience? Use Google Adsense! With Google AdSense, you get a second revenue stream as you continue to scale your business. AdSense basically allows you to create ad blocks that you can use throughout your site that other sites can pay to utilize. You can also select payments based on per ad in a variety of manners such as through CPM. Applying this method, you get paid a flat fee per thousand website pageviews for a specific ad. The rates can range between $1 to $3 and this rate can go higher based on niche categories. Another way which you can do this is through CPC which is cost-per-click. This way, you get paid each time an ad is clicked on your site. The rates for this vary between one industry to the other.

- AdThrive

Getting money from Adsense is slightly tough, but if you have a good website, Adsense can give you a second revenue stream no doubt. What if you're only making a few dollars in ads and only have about 1,000 website visitors? You can also use AdThrive to optimize your ads so you get better performance. AdThrive delves deep into your analytics to understand the advertisers who have the best performance on your site. From this, you can see higher CTRs on your ads and this will enable you to generate more revenue.

- InfusionSoft

InfusionSoft is a paid software and a little on the pricey end, but it is a powerful tool to use for any marketer and manager. Its finest feature is the automation that makes extremely efficient marketing campaigns for you. InfusionSoft is a robust yet costly email marketing tool that would benefit any small business looking towards reaching out to a bigger audience. The startup fee for this software is at $2,000. After this, maintenance would cost anywhere between $199 to $599 a month depending on the package you choose.

In brief, InfusionSoft saves you plenty of time. For first time users, it takes a little while to learn how to use the system and set it up according to your needs. But once setup is completed, you are pretty much set up for a smooth ride. InfusionSoft is renowned for its high deliverability rates and its ability to scale no matter what the size of the campaign.

- Keyhole

Keyhole offers a detailed analysis of the hashtags that you use for your marketing campaign. Instead of randomly using hashtags with your campaigns, Keyhole enables you to track and analyze hashtags in real time, shows you how influential it is, as well as its engagement, reach and popularity. The trial is free, but paid versions start at$132 to $799 a month. Let's face it- marketing campaigns nowadays thrive on hashtags. Not only can you track hashtags, but you can also get analytics by account, keywords, mentions and URL. This is a useful tool to have if you are always working on marketing campaigns targeting heavy social media users.

- Buzzsumo

Buzzsumo enables marketers to source the most shared content on specific topics and websites. Marketers can also refine lists according to the type of content such as blog posts, news items, or just infographics. The advanced feature includes 'monitoring' and 'influencers' that marketers can use to get ahead of the competition. The free version of Buzzsumo gives you limited results. However, the pro version starter plan is ideal for small businesses and bloggers, as it costs $99/month. But if you want something deeper and significant, then the Advanced feature at $299/month comes with API access and many more incredible features.

Content marketers would love this because it helps in searching for trending topics and subjects on the internet easier and plus, it allows content creators to analyze headlines for their effectiveness. Buzzsumo helps content marketers understand how to create the next viral topic.

- CoSchedule

CoSchedule is a software that helps you plan, organize and manage your marketing campaigns, your content and your strategies. Any marketing campaign needs to be planned and executed according to schedule, and with CoSchedule, you can streamline this process easily. CoShedule works great with Chrome, Google Docs, Wordpress and Evernote too! Coschedule ranges from $15 per month for personal use to $600 per month for larger agency users. Coshedule allows you to stay organized and it saves time. It is excellent for large companies or small agencies to manage deadlines, share notes, stay up on to their day to day tasks and get updates on campaign progress. Timelines are easier to manage, any alerts are prompted by CoSchedule.

- Pingdom Website Speed Test

Website speed is a crucial element in retaining a user's visit to your site. Website speed is one of the fastest ways to improve your SEO rankings and increase conversion rates. With Pingdom's, marketers can test their website speed, and it also gives a free report that gives you an in-depth analysis of your site as well as tips to improve it. The test itself is free however for a full on website monitoring service; it will cost you anywhere from $13.95 to $454 per month.

Full-time monitoring is essential and useful for large websites that receive plenty of traffic. A few more minutes of downtime or crash can cost you revenue as well as traffic. You can save a lot of money by investing in a monthly plan with Pingdom to continuously check your websites' status, give you alerts and monitor and report on site speed.

- Canva

With easy to use designing software available to us, most of our company's basic design materials can be made ourselves because let's face it: not everyone can afford a graphic designer on a retainer basis. If Adobe Photoshop and Illustrator is too complicated to us, then Canva is an easier alternative that makes design easy and fast. Canva has templates that are created especially for social media sharing and posting, and these templates are stunning. A few clicks here and there and you have eye-popping visual.

If you use its cloud-based software, it costs nothing. But there are premium features that come, and it is a 'pay-as-you-go 'method. If you feel your business needs constant designing but hiring a graphic designer is too much, then opt for Canva For Work. It has advanced features and a variety of other tools that you can utilize for a mere monthly subscription of $12.95.

Great visual design can create a huge impact on your target market so if you are embarking on a big marketing campaign, do not skimp on hiring a graphic designer. But if you need visual content quickly and it's something that you can easily put together quickly, then Canva will help you make your content look stunning.

Chapter 13. The Top 9 Mistakes You Shouldn't Make in Affiliate Marketing

Everyone makes mistakes and so can affiliate marketers. Mistakes are more common when you are just a beginner because that is the stage when you perform all the trial and error experiments with your campaigns and strategies. And that is exactly how you become a pro gradually. It is true that a mistake is what makes you wise but at times, these mistakes can be a costly affair and so are better off avoided.

Mistake 1 – Wrong product choice

Affiliate marketing campaigns cover every possible product on this plant and the product need not always be something physical. It can be digital too. But with so many options also comes the need to make the right choice. But can making the wrong choice impact your affiliate marketing strategy? Yes, it can. And so you need to be careful while selecting the product as this is one of your basic steps as an affiliate marketer. This can be your defining moment towards success, so don't rush it.

Your niche should be something that will drive you and inspire you to make good content. You shouldn't be forcing yourself to sit in front of your laptop and do research on products to promote. It should be your passion. When you are inspired from your niche, you can easily devise several other marketing strategies and activities around it. Moreover, the passion might take you to such a level that your work becomes even more authentic and unique and that is exactly what will help you to stand out from the rest of the affiliate marketers. A simple search on Google about ideas on affiliate marketing niches will bring you thousands of results but picking something randomly never works.

One very common mistake that several budding affiliate marketers make is choosing a niche just because it brings more money. You need to understand one very simple thing. No matter how prominent or cool the niche is, you will never be able to make it big if you yourself are not interested in it. Believe it or not, nobody in the world is a natural when it comes to affiliate marketer. Every big affiliate marketer of today started out with something they love and then they spent days and nights researching and sharpening their skills. But if the product choice is wrong, you will just feel like a slave doing this just for the sake of money and not because you really want to.

Mistake 2 – Promoting too many products right from the beginning

This is another mistake which people make but don't really see the fault in it. When you are just starting out in this field, there will be a temptation to include as many products as you can and start promoting all of them. Don't do that. The default approach towards affiliate marketing for any new person in this field is being over-enthusiastic and over-ambitious. But this will ultimately lead to stress and demotivation when you have to figure out proper strategies for all these products. You will quickly become less and less enthusiastic and drop the entire strategy altogether. It is easy to get distracted when you have too much on your plate and you will not have any time for yourself or for your family.

The value you are putting in starts lowering down and this, ultimately, brings down the number of sales. So, if you want to be smart, then focus less on the quantity and more on the quality because that is how you climb the ladder of success. Pick a handful of products which you personally feel good about and would love to promote. Research extensively on them and focus all your energy onto those products. When you commit your brainstorming capacity and focus on a single product at a time, you will come up with better ideas and statistics show that you will also find it easier to convert your promotions into actual sales.

If you are thinking that approaching affiliate marketing in this manner will do you no good and will only shun your growth, then think again. There is no harm in proceeding one product at a time. Why cause havoc by trying your hand out at many things when you can make each product a success and then proceed? Every campaign is different from all aspects and thus, they need individual attention. So, you need to provide the campaigns with what they need and success is not far.

Mistake 3 – Only trying to sell and not help

With affiliate marketing, people often develop a mindset that is all about selling and not actually helping the audience with any information. If this continues, you will gradually start losing the audience that you have. Don't let sales become your only priority. Yes, you will have the tendency to do it, but remind yourself about long-term profitability. The mindset of making profits only will not give you poor results but also generate mediocre content. Good-quality content is what you should focus on. When your content is good, audience will follow and so will the sales.

Your writing should be focused on how the readers can benefit from it. Every feature should be explained in detail and think about all the probable questions that might pop up in the minds of the readers. Once you have figured the questions out, make a separate FAQ section with every piece of content and answer those questions there so that your audience is not left with any confusion. Keep friction at bay. The placement of banner ads can be sometimes frustrating to the audience. So place them accordingly so that they do not drive your readers so angry that they have reached a point of no-return.

Whenever you implement some sort of outbound sales tactic, some consequence will come. It is up to you to decide which ones you really want and which ones are not worth the hassle.

Mistake 4 – Poor quality website

This is another mistake that affiliate marketers make. Your content is definitely important but your content is not all about what you write. It is also about the platform. When your website quality is low, you will notice your traffic decreasing which results in a low volume of sales. If you are not an experienced web designer, don't worry because you don't have to be. No one is telling you to be perfect from the beginning. But with the resources that are available in today's world, making a good website is way easier than ever before. WordPress is one of the best places to start because of their user-friendly approach.

User experience matters a lot if you want to retain your audience. If there are too many ads on your webpage or if the page is not responsive enough, then your audience might simply migrate to some other page providing the same information. A messy template is also one of the many reasons which can scare off your visitors because your website might appear to be too complex for them. When you lose audience because of these cases, there are very low chances of gaining them back because no matter how much improvement you make, those people will remember your website for the bad experience they had.

You can understand this well when you compare it with shopping. Shoppers always prefer those shops which are clean and tidy and have everything arranged in a proper manner. They are even likely to spend more in such shops. But they will not visit an overcrowded mall because they cannot figure out anything over there. So, some of the things that you should make sure while building the website are –

- The website should be easily navigated
- Every section should be properly categorized and easy to find
- The website should be responsive
- The calls to action should be prominent and clear
- Every page should have only one call to action
- The on-site elements should be properly highlighted on the webpages and the design should be chosen accordingly

It's true that building a website can be overwhelming but when done with patience, it is not something impossible.

Mistake 5 – Content that is regular and of high-quality

Have you every though about what your product is as an affiliate marketer? Well, the answer is quite simple – it is your content. Every affiliate marketer wants to get more sales but in order to make your audience, you will first need to have good content. If readers find your content to be credible and valuable, they will automatically want to rely on your advice when they want to buy a product. The common misconception that almost every affiliate marketer has is that if you have 10 mediocre posts then it is equivalent to one great post. But this is a lie. It never happens that way.

No matter what type of content you produce, whether they are posts on product comparisons or product reviews, your sales will be directly or indirectly affected by the quality of your content. If your content is not actionable or insightful, then there is no use of publishing content at all. Consider yourself as the buyer every time you compose a new post and then think about the fact whether the post would have been useful to you or not. The universal rule of getting any person hooked to your writing is to make your content interesting.

The first step to composing a new post is to decide the topic. Once that is done, you need to research keywords. Find keywords that are relevant to your topic and have less competition. This has to be done if you want to outrank the competition that is already present. You should also check the word count of the posts that are ranking high on the first-page results. Then, set that word count as a benchmark for your own posts. Don't forget to include images in your posts because it is normally seen that posts with images automatically rank higher than posts that do not have any images at all. Lastly, be regular with your posts and don't make your audience wait too long for the next post.

Mistake 6 – Not keeping an eye on the performance of your website

Not making use of a tracking tool is another of the common mistakes made by affiliate marketers. You cannot simply have a glance at your website and say whether it is performing good or bad. You need to have access to advanced tools with which you can study the metrics. If you do not track your data, you will not be able to optimize it and without these two things marketing is simply nothing. Whatever strategies you are implementing or whatever tweaks you are making to your strategies or campaigns will have an effect and these tracking tools will help you study that effect. You need to be able to recognize all the patterns that are working out in your favor. Google Analytics is the best tool to monitor all aspects of the website performance but if you want, you can use any such similar tool as well.

Does your website have a good speed? This is another important aspect that is highly overlooked. Studies have proved that whenever a website takes longer than 2 seconds to load, the audience bounce rate automatically increases by a whopping 50%. You have to keep it in mind that everyone is impatient. Everyone wants to see the content now or never. If you keep your audience waiting, they will simply find another site that won't be delaying them. Mode of content delivery, large file size and response times of the servers are some of the usual reasons of a slow website.

If you are facing problems with your file size, then you can use any of the online tools to compress your image. But you should keep in mind that the quality of the image should not be compromised. Taking these small steps can help you towards reducing the load time of your website.

Mistake 7 – Neglecting content readability

As already mentioned, readers are impatient. So, you have to take every measure possible to make your content user-friendly and readable. Whenever your content is hard to understand or the sentences are confusing, the tolerance level of your readers will start decreasing. The font size you use also matters. You need to choose the size that is not too big or too small. Avoid anything that is below 16pt. But the font size is not the only determining factor acting here. Your font style will matter too. Avoid fonts that are not clear. Moreover, prefer a serif font when it comes to constructing paragraphs.

Don't make your sentences long. Keep them short and crisp. A sentence should contain approximately 25 words because according to research, anything more than that becomes confusing to several people.

Paragraphs should follow the same rules. Don't make them too long.

If you don't know the meaning of a word, then don't include it. An average reader prefers a grade eight or seven level of readability. Even those readers who have high academic qualifications prefer the readability level to the one mentioned before.

Mistake 8 – Ignoring SEO

Ignoring the basic aspects of SEO can definitely cost you a lot. If you do not include the proper meta descriptions and title tags, it will be impossible for people to find your content. And the sole motive of publishing these posts is to drive traffic so you should not forget SEO. The title tag should be compelling so that readers are bound to click on your post. If you are using WordPress, then the Yoast SEO plugin is a very good option to optimize your content and make it SEO-friendly.

To establish a proper hierarchy within your content, internal links are something you should implement.

Mistake 9 – Not making evergreen content

Something trendy comes up every other day on the internet and it can become difficult to keep up at times. But there will always be those topics which are evergreen and you should definitely include them on your website. Now, it is true that these topics have an immense amount of competition because everyone is writing on them. Moreover, they might also not be of much value to you as an affiliate.

But, when implemented correctly, these evergreen posts have high link building value. Sustainable content in the long-form layout can also be made more credible by adding phrases like '2019 updated edition' and your audience will automatically become interested in the updates.

If you think your content has any of the above-mentioned mistakes, then there is no harm in revising it again. Make the appropriate changes and then hit the Publish button.

Chapter 14. Create Your Affiliate Marketing Plan

Attracting website visitors is the next step to take once you have your website, content, and you have signed up for affiliate programs. Without traffic, you will not be able to sell anything.

What types of people do you want to attract?

After you get accepted to an affiliate network or program, study the product that you are selling. More importantly, learn the target audience of your product. Start by making a list the basic information of the target demographics. You may include the age bracket and the gender of the usual buyers of the product. Also, include the common interest of the buyers.

If there are obvious online properties where the buyers may spend their time, you should also list them down. This will make it easier for you to organize the information when you start developing your traffic gathering strategies.

When you identify your target audience, make sure that you are targeting the decision makers in the buying process. Identifying the decision makers can be tricky for most people. When selling engagement rings, for example, the product is designed for women while the marketing is targeted towards men.

The same goes for selling toys. The products are designed for kids. However, usually, the parents buy the toys for the kids. Therefore, you are targeting your marketing efforts to the parents.

Two Fundamental Attraction Methods

There are two general ways to attract people towards your affiliate links, organic and paid methods.

The Organic Method

The organic method refers to authority and trust building strategies that create long-term relationships with visitors. With this method, you are converting visitors of your website into fans.

To make this method work, you will need a constant stream of content that your visitors find entertaining or useful. Obviously, the content that you share should always be related to the product or service that you are offering. If you already have a popular website before you start affiliate marketing, you should find affiliate products or services that are compatible with your website's theme.

You could then use various online marketing techniques to drive traffic towards your website. The most popular among these methods are social media marketing and search marketing.

After that, make your visitors subscribe to you in their network of choice. If most of your visitors come from Facebook, for instance, you could use a pop-up to encourage people to like your page. By doing so, the visitor gets to see the content you share on your Facebook page.

You could also encourage them to sign up for your email newsletters. Instead of encouraging Facebook likes, you could ask them to sign up for your free newsletter instead.

Your goal is to create a relationship with your website visitors by providing valuable content and communicating with them in your various media channels. To do this, you need to show up in your visitors' feeds or email regularly. However, you should not just email them promotional posts all the time. Instead, you should limit your promotional content to 5-10% of the content you share via email and social media.

Try to share only important content in these channels to make people go back to your website. Eventually, your visitors may develop enough trust in you to follow your advice. When this happens, they will voluntarily click on the affiliate links that you promote and start using the products or services that you recommend.

The Paid Method

For some people, this process may seem too long. They want to try to hasten the process by using paid methods to gather traffic. Paid traffic may speed up the process if you have the right targeting tools and information. Unfortunately, most beginners are not aware of how to limit their ads only to their target audience. As a result, their ads end up being shown to people who may not be interested in their products. Their cost-per-click rises. The ad campaign ends up costing too much.

When using paid campaigns, the affiliate marketer's goal is to make the profit of the sales outscore the cost of the ads. This will be difficult to do if the cost of marketing is too high.

Refine your process

As a beginner in affiliate marketing, you should stick to the organic method for now. Build an online property that establishes trust with visitors and focuses on your chosen topic or niche. You can then test various ways of pitching your affiliate products to the visitors you attract.

With a combination of testing and implementation, you can increase the rate of conversion of visitors into buyers.

Even as a beginner, you can already start trying out paid options for advertising. You could start with simple goals like increasing your email subscribers or getting more social media followers. However, because you are just starting out, start with a small budget to minimize the risk of your online campaigns. Your goal in your early ad campaigns is to learn how to refine ad targeting.

You should also read up on how to run online marketing campaigns. The best practices for implementing these campaigns vary depending on your industry and your overall marketing strategy. For now, you could aim to practice your techniques and find the strategies that work for your own campaigns.

Where do you get traffic using the organic method?

To get traffic to click to your affiliate links, you need to know where your target audience spends most of their time online. These days, most internet users spend the majority of their time on social media apps and websites. However, some of your target audience may also be present in other web properties. Here are some of the methods you can use when researching:

Use Google to search your niche keywords

The easiest way to learn about where most of your target audience spends most of their time is by searching a popular keyword in your niche. Let's say you want to sell travel backpacks to men. To sell this type of product, you need to advertise on online properties that attract male travelers. You could also look for mountaineering related websites. With this in mind, you can search the following keywords:

- 'Best travel membership sites for men'
- 'Best mountaineering websites for men'

If you use these key phrases on Google, you will find list articles to popular websites that may offer content related to your product. Try to find active online communities with hundreds of thousands of members. You could also look for small blogs that attract a large amount of people.

Look at ranking websites

You could also use the data of ranking websites like Alexa.com when researching about traffic sources. You want to find the most popular online communities related to your niche. If you plan on marketing to a specific country outside of the US, use the country filter when looking for the most popular websites.

After finding these traffic sources, you should list down ways on how you can promote your own content on them. If it's a Q and A or a forum website, for example, you could aim to provide helpful answers to other people's questions. You could put links to your website in your profile or your forum signature. You could also include them in the answers if you have content in your website that is part of the solution to their questions.

Most of your answers will be crawled by Google and you may get a decent amount of traffic if you answer enough questions. Don't do this as an SEO strategy because most of these websites have a no-follow attribute to their links. Instead, just focus on three or four forums or Q and A websites where you can be a helpful member.

For starters, you can start with websites like Quora and Reddit. You could also identify forums that are specific to the niche you have chosen.

Look inside each big social network

Most social networks and apps cannot be searched using Google. When looking for communities related to your product inside these networks, you should search from within the network. When using Facebook, for example, look for pages related to the product or service you are offering. Learning about the popular pages and groups in your chosen community will help when creating your marketing strategy later in the process.

Getting traffic through search engine marketing

Aside from websites and apps, you should also consider search engine marketing to gain traffic for your affiliate marketing business. Search engine marketing refers to the practice of competing to reach the top of the search result pages of Google and other search engines for your selected keywords. This form of marketing requires you to accomplish certain tasks that improve the ranking of your website in your chosen search engines. The tasks that you need to do range from improving your website, creating and marketing content and interacting with other website owners.

The amount of traffic that you get from this method depends on the quality of keywords that you rank for. If the keywords that you want to rank for is extremely competitive, you may have difficulty getting traffic because other websites with better content dominate the top spot. You can use tools like Google Ad Words Keyword Planner to find high traffic sales-related keywords with low competition.

Keeping people's attention

Marketers online are always fighting over the attention of internet users. After attracting your target audience to your page or your website, the next step is to make them stick around.

If you have a website, your goal is to keep your visitors returning. You can do this in multiple ways. One way is by promising them with valuable content. If people need the types of content that you offer, they will try to remember your website on their own. However, you should make it easier for them to remember your website through various subscription tools.

These days, social media seems to be the best subscription tool to keep visitors coming back. You can create a Facebook page to represent your website inside Facebook and encourage your website visitors to like your page. If they choose to do it, they may see the content that you share when they use Facebook. If they click on it, they will be directed back to your website. The same strategy could be used with Instagram, Twitter, and other social networks.

Another way to keep users coming back is by using email marketing. Most websites encourage you to subscribe to their email newsletter. This subscription is usually free. It only requires you only to enter your name and email address. In return, you will get free content straight to your email address. With emails now available in smartphones, this method is becoming even more effective.

The emails could contain anything from short articles to sales pitches. Ultimately, it invites people to go back to the website.

Another way to make people come back is by encouraging them to comment on your content. If they do comment, they have the option to put in their email address so that they will be notified whenever somebody replies to their comments.

Conclusion

Now you know that Affiliate Marketing is a way of making money as an intermediary. Marketers make a commission from a sale or a referral when a visitor to their site clicks on a link that directs them to a product or page online. Furthermore, contrary to what most people would think, Affiliate Marketing has been around for a very long time and did not start after the invention of the Internet.

In the recent past, the Affiliate Marketing business has enjoyed extraordinary growth, and experts are foreseeing that the upward trend will continue. One of the best news about this trend is that about 81% of online sales have involved an affiliate marketer and according to a study by Forrester Consulting, by 2020, the industry's spending in the United States will exceed $6.8 billion.

The core concept of Affiliate Marketing is that it is performance-based, it has an element of independence, the partnership element, and universality. The core players involved in Affiliate Marketing include:

- The merchant/advertiser, brand, or retailer

- The consumer
- The affiliate marketer/publisher
- The affiliate network
- The affiliate program

In terms of payments, Affiliates need to think about the percentage of the total sales they will get, how the parties deal with reversals and the locking periods involved. Furthermore, the incentives available for the marketer, how many times an affiliate will expect to receive payment over a specified period and how much money an affiliate marketer should have to make before withdrawing his or her earnings are important.

An affiliate Marketer needs to capitalize on the advantages that are the result of search engine optimization, which he or she will need to learn how to use the right keywords, define the ideal length of the posts, and how to go about On-Page and off-page optimization. These days, it is impossible to make it without Mobile Optimization because the number of mobile Internet users is rising every day, and so is the size of the online mobile market.

Interested Affiliate Marketers need to know how to use Social Media to market their products, and the main strategies most successful marketers out there are using to continue to succeed. In essence, these Marketers have to identify the main sources of traffic and the process of keeping people coming to their pages. Furthermore, so many marketers have made mistakes that future marketers do not need to repeat since it is possible to learn from their mistakes. One more thing a beginner Affiliate Marketer should take time to consider is the niche he or she will invest in and the Affiliate program ideal for his or her needs.

The next step is to implement all the instructions and suggestions in this book because the proper application of its contents will ensure success.